STRETCHING THE THIN BLUE

POLICING AMERICA IN TIMES OF HEIGHTENED THREAT

By

DR. ROSS L. RIGGS

LEADERS IN GLOBAL PUBLISHING

Published by Motivational Press, Inc.
1777 Aurora Road
Melbourne, Florida, 32935
www.MotivationalPress.com

Manufactured in the United States of America.

ISBN: 978-1-62865-455-4

PROLOGUE

Joni Mitchell a singer song-writer of the sixties and seventies wrote a very personal song that was performed by songstress Judy Collins on an album titled 'Wildflowers' under the name *Both Sides Now*. It had been first released in 1969 by Mitchell on 'Clouds' based on the first topic of the song. The final refrain goes like this:

I've looked at life from both sides now

From win and lose and still somehow

It's life's illusions I recall

really don't know life at all

Policing in the west, in America particularly, has witnessed dramatic changes over nearly two and a half centuries. Is it possible these changes are nothing more than the illusions some portray them to be? Based on Dr. Riggs' most recent research, the 21st

Century and its times of greatly heightened threats to Americans and America, Dr. Riggs contends that it is time for every American to be part of the local solution.

Citizens must decide to be prepared to stand shoulder to shoulder with some of America's finest to protect the American way of life, in whatever way it is defined in each locale. It is time, too, for America's law enforcement to re-define their thin-blue line, stretch it if they must, to include the new breed of *Citizen Centurions* that step to the fore. **Specifically chosen citizens alongside highly trained professional police officers are the**

keystone to stopping terrorists. The challenges terrorism brings to America's shores, requires America's strongest resource - her people, all of them, united to a common cause.

Stretching the Thin Blue Line: Policing America In Times of Heightened Threat is the exposition of a multi-pronged strategic plan to combat terrorism. The plan is written by a retired Chief of Police. It is written for implementation by American law enforcement agencies working alongside local American citizens, to protect the American homeland against terrorists and others who would seek to destroy her. Can other agencies in other societies around the world use this strategy? To quote a Canadian hockey coach, *"Who knows?"* [ii] That is not its purpose. If someone else can take it and adapt it to their culture, their communities, and their people then more power to them. Its purpose however is for the U.S. here and now. It is not even designed for the federal level in America, although the federal level plays an important role; and it will only partially work at the state level when the state law enforcement is divided into sub-units that are working in localized areas consistently. It is time for local law enforcement in America's cities, towns, townships, counties and boroughs to step up to the plate.

Clear your minds of ideas that this is the same old programs re-packaged. If you are thinking that way then put the book back on the shelf and go pick up a mystery novel you can read at your leisure. This text will cause you to rethink officer deployment, reconsider the use of civilians and volunteers and even retired cops. This text is about no long-playing defense when it comes to terrorism – it's time to take the ball to their side of the field and play some serious offense. We do that by taking back our homes which begins with fathers taking real spiritual leadership roles in their families.

Together we are going to re-take homes and build them into the castles that they should be. Some of the best advice to young men and women planning to get married and starting a family includes, making your home your castle; making sure the moat is full and the drawbridge is up so that you can protect it at *all* costs from *all* who would seek to destroy it. It is not, however, a matter of isolationism or withdrawing into the castle and again play only defense. It is to protect within the castle that which is most precious so that the noble blue knights who venture out to battle can rest assured that no matter their personal outcome – everything at home is secure. In the movie based on Seal Team Six, the team leader admonished the team that no one goes on mission until they have everything squared away at home. There cannot be a divided mind and heart when it is time to face the enemy.

Once we have retaken our castles, then we will re-draw the thin blue line and not only stretch it with people we perhaps never considered before, we are going to gain a momentum aided by a majority that allows the full power and weight of the U.S. government and her military to come down on the problem when local resources just aren't enough. By then, the citizens of this great land who have had enough of the political correctness and enough of the inclusiveness of anything and everything regardless of how hurtful it is to our homes and our society will be speaking in unison.

When that happens, if the politicians sitting behind little desks in semi-circle galleries in Washington decide they want to impede the citizen's rights to take legal action to protect their homes and communities, Americans will send them a very clear and cohesive message. It will be a message to which those in Congress will have to listen. Finally, the majority will be speaking as one voice.

As families become more stable, it will be possible to focus on a primary issue and that is securing America's borders (notice it is plural). Once the borders are truly secure then Americans can get a handle on who is supposed to be here and who isn't. That is when we open up very special doors at the borders – the ones marked EXIT! Citizens acting lawfully with their local law enforcement are finally going to take a stand with a strategic plan and then we will ask our elected officials to 'lead-follow-or get out of the way.'

Joni Mitchel and Joan Collins wondered if life is an illusion. The message for everyone today is: *The illusion is the idea that there are groups of bullies and thugs who think they can make us afraid to enter buildings or airliners. It is the bullies and the thugs who are suffering from an illusion.*

What we have as Americans is real. Those of us who name the Name of Christ, (that is, we call ourselves Christians) and who also call ourselves Americans have an obligation. If we truly believe that God is the One and only person who controls destiny then we must ask God to bless America. We do not ask Him to do so because she deserves blessing; but because the Triune God desires to bless those who will humble themselves before Him. It is also our obligation then to humble ourselves before our Heavenly Father. Those of us who claim His Name must no longer make a halting endeavor to soft-sell our faith. We will follow the scripture's admonition written by Paul, "Humble yourselves under the mighty hand of God so that He might exalt you in due time."

The law enforcement strategies are real. The methodologies for defeating terrorism are real, the need to take back our homes is real; but without that final piece of God's blessing, complete success will never fully come. Can non-believers use this book? Absolutely. Can non-evangelical believers use these strategies? Absolutely. Don't throw the baby out with the bathwater, as the old 'Mountain Wisdom' puts it. Take a chance and read something that will challenge your thinking. If you want to take a risk that somebody who is a Christian and a cop might just have been given the ability to put a strategy together that might just work, then take this book on over to the check out and buy it and then *read it!* If you hate the idea of a Christian giving you ideas on how to deploy your officers or if you don't want a Christian to tell you about how you can re-take the leadership role in your home, then put the book back on the shelf, or get it and don't read those chapters – focus on the law enforcement strategies. Whatever you decide to do with the book, I hope (and pray) that if you are in a decision-making role in a community, in a police agency or a citizen at home who is ready to get involved that you really will take this book and take it to heart.

Some may think, because of my reference to Christianity, this book narrowly will define terrorists as non-white, non-Christian people. Allow me to point out here first that it is likely most Christians in the world are not Caucasian. The vast growth of the Christian church in places like Asia is just one example of why this could be so. If one assumes, because a book is written by a Christian in America he must be white and therefore sees all terrorists as non-Christian, non-white, speaks only to the presuppositions of the reader and is ludicrous. According to Meriam Webster, (https://www.merriam-webster.com/dictionary/terrorism), a terrorist is one who employs "the systematic use of terror especially as a means of coercion". Other definitions include the line *to advance a political agenda.* Another is simply, "any act taken by a group or individual, whereas the act is used to Intimidate or coerce the non-profit organization, its employees, or affiliates; AND used to Influence the policy of the non-profit or any government authority by intimidation or coercion; AND affects the conduct of the non-profit or any government authority by the act."[lii]

Over the history of the U.S., terrorists have had labels including: Left-wing Anti-Government; White Supremacists; Puerto Rican Nationalists, Palestinians, Black Radicals, Right-wing Extremists, Anti-Government; Anti-Abortionists, and Islamist Extremists. Many of these have faded to history. No doubt others will come. Today, the largest threat for acts of terrorism in the United States comes from those associated with al Qaeda, ISIS, ISIL and other Muslim-Extremists who have openly declared war on the U.S. Some are white converts to Islam; most are non-white.

Law enforcement can use the tools in this book to combat any new terrorist threat. I do believe, however, that truly born-again followers of Christ, who come in all colors of the skin, cannot follow the teachings of the Bible and commit any grievous acts of terror against other human beings. It is against all of Christ's teachings. Any group, such as the anti-abortionists who claim to be Christian are fooling only themselves to their own demise. Terrorists are real. Our times today in America are violent.

The enemy is on our doorstep. You can hunker down in the house, run out the back door to try to escape, or you can open that front door and send the enemy to meet the Judge.

It is time to stop being afraid.

i *www.jonimitchell.com/music/song.cfm?id=83*

ii Collins, Bradley

iii http://ema.ohio.gov/PreparednessGrants_
SecurityGrantsforNonProfits.aspx

Chapter 1

American Police

Defining Police in America

In a basic police certification class, nearly forty years ago, the class of recruits, among whom I was numbered, were required to study a brief section on the history of policing. Discussions included Roman Centurions, Shire Reeves in medieval England, and whether copper buttons on English Bobby's coats were the source of the early American terminology 'coppers' or if 'constables on patrol' became 'cops', 'Peelers' and 'Bobbies' from Sir Robert Peele - all of which served little purpose in getting the recruits prepared for policing in America in the 70's and 80's and beyond. We were actually instructed to carry a role of dimes in case, while on foot patrol, the 'call light' on the telephone pole downtown came on and we had to find a phone booth to call headquarters! Certainly, it is important to understand the history of a profession, to understand the foundations upon which it is built; but this information was superfluous to the purpose of the training. It was fluff and what we needed was solid, basic knowledge that would help us go home safely at the end of our shifts. One of the principle issues, however, which was very appropriate had to do with knowing your community. This is a central premise to the role of this book.

Whether it came to knowing the city streets, the local businesses, the townspeople or the troublemakers, the key point in each of them was that a first-hand knowledge of each aspect would not only make us better police officers, it would better serve our community. There was, in those days, a large amount of talk about unionizing police agencies and unionizing had a great deal to do with the residency requirements that cities maintained for their safety services personnel. The belief was that a police officer who knew the community and was part of the daily life of the community would have a stake in the city. Having a stake, in part because of their work, but also because their families were growing up there, would give them even more incentive to be better cops. The opposing argument was that truly professional officers would provide excellent service no matter where they lived and it would be safer for their families. It is true professional officers will give all they have to their community. They can never, however, have the intimate knowledge of those people who are their citizens unless they are one of them day in and day out with their families there and their children in the schools. Is it appropriate to give up part of that knowledge for the well-being of the officer? That is an argument that continues to be waged.

Jesus told a parable of the hired shepherd who did not own or truly care about the sheep he tended just for pay. That shepherd would run at the sight of danger. A good shepherd knows his sheep and cares for them, Jesus said; he will stand strong in the face of danger and go out to search even for one out of a hundred that becomes lost. The focus of this book is about the local community's capability to thwart an act of terrorism. The local shepherds not only know their sheep, they also know where all the risks are when those sheep are grazing. That knowledge allows the shepherd to avoid danger. It also allows him to anticipate trouble before it happens because he knows where to look. This is a study of American cops – the shepherds of their local flocks.

As the study of *American cops* begins, allow a short excursion into what some might term political correctness and others might see it as more *superfluous fluff.* This book is about *policing in America.* When I travel to different parts of the sphere we call 'Earth' there is really only one group of people that have ever called me on my use of the term 'Americans' when referring to the United States of America and her resident citizenry. Everywhere in the world, it seems, when someone refers to the *ugly Americans* they are conspicuously meaning those who call the red and white stripes, thirteen in all, and fifty white stars brightly contrasted on a field of blue *their* flag. They are referring to those who reside primarily between 49° 23'4.1" N and 24° 31'15" N latitude(s) to 66° 57' W and 124° 46' W longitude(s); as well as those who live in the Pacific who brave the harsh winters of Honolulu or the brazen hot sun of Point Barrow, Alaska (or was it...?) Only my Canadian friends have ever pointed out that they, too, are technically *Americans.* I remind them, good naturedly, that there is a primary difference. One is a land of free *citizens* of a Republic and the other consists of *subjects* to the British Crown and they need to get beyond it. In any event, my generalization about *American* policing focuses on police living or working primarily in the fifty states of the United States of America. There are some distinctions between street cops in the Bronx, tribal police in Alaska or North Dakota, and the border police along the Rio Grande. I know cops from most of the states and just as our shared blood links cops around the world, certainly the shared heritage of America brings together a uniqueness shared by all of the *American cops* of which I write. I am very mindful of the thousands of Canadian cops who share a blood affinity with us and we see them at every funeral for a brother or sister killed in the line of duty, so I am not demeaning them in any way. The Canadian friends with whom I take issue have never been *on the job.* So, in deference to my Canadian friends, as far as I am aware there has never been an *American* cop named Dudley Doright.

AMERICA'S NIGHT WATCHMEN MOVE WEST

The only possible way that Americans may be able to stop the next terrorist attack on American soil is for the local communities, *their police and the citizens who are closest to whatever the next Ground Zero will be,* to agree that together they will create a new design for law enforcement. Police and specifically chosen local citizens must covenant to work hand in hand to stop the advancement of terrorism in our country. This cannot be a re-warming of old *programs* that were designed as feel-good citizen and cop interactions or those that were somewhat effective crime deterrent tools. The *Thin Blue Line* is traditionally defined as a local law enforcement that serves as the last line of defense between civilization and anarchy. The times in which we live require a radical redrawing, a stretching if you will, of the *thin blue line.*

If such a new line is to be drawn, then it must be sketched with an understanding of who are *American Police.* For that understanding, it is necessary to go back in time across the last two centuries and beyond to learn the incredible chemistry that combined to conceive the American law enforcement officer and to watch the transformations that have taken place across the decades, even as the world around them grew at exponential speed.

I encourage you now to open your mind to envision the life of the local police officer from the earliest days of the *American experiment.*

Rooted in the struggle for independence and a hard life in a wilderness fraught with danger, rugged individualism has become a by-word for colonial and early post-Revolutionary War America. What was born in the cities of the East as both lamplighters and night watchmen, mostly on guard for fires that could spread out of control in minutes and devastate entire communities, became the guardians in the night against those who would steal the public peace and just about anything else they could get their hands on. The lamplighters and fire watchers began as volunteers. They held a sense of civic pride in their ability to watch over their towns and the people in them to keep them and their livelihoods safe. It is that same sense of local care that will enable today's new 'night watchers' the new *Centurions* to forestall a terrorist attack on their home soil.

As America grew, a special spirit brought some of these very fine men with families west and a less then special spirit drew, too, the less scrupulous who would seek their fortunes off the hard work of others. The former saw the need for men to protect and serve those with whom they shared their vision. That mindset has been part of the American police psyche through the Westward expansion and the early days of the territorial sheriffs and the early U.S. Marshals Service. Historically, some of the best cops would have also been really good criminals. As a matter of fact, some were. In America's West during the latter part of the 19th century, some of the local sheriffs had previous careers as criminals, a few considerably more successful than others. Perhaps that je ne sais quoi that creates such a fine line between the law keepers and the law breakers is also what makes the good cops able to foresee how a criminal might act and thus catch him. The new Centurions will use that same tactic in capturing the would-be terrorist before he can strike. A few examples may help to make the point more clearly.

Henry Newton Brown rode with Billy the Kid's gang, known for rustling cattle. Brown decided to stay in Texas when the Kid headed for Mexico. Not long before heading to Mexico, though, William Bonney, aka, Billy the Kid was involved in the Lincoln County War. On February 18, 1878 - The Lincoln County War began in New Mexico between two groups of wealthy business-men, the ranchers and the Lincoln County general store. William Bonney fought alongside the ranchers in a dispute over the seizure of horses as a payment of an outstanding debt. It is possible that Henry Brown was with Bonney during that time. Later, Brown became a deputy sheriff in Oldham County, Texas where he was eventually fired for picking fights with drunks. He became an as-sistant marshal in Caldwell, Texas until resuming his stealing and was involved in a shoot-out during a bank robbery. Marshal Brown who had brought an uneasy order to the rough town with his quick trigger finger was lynched by an angry mob in 1884, just eight years after the Lincoln County War. Brown was barely 27 years old.

Old age did not come often to western outlaws or lawmen. Brown understood the mindset of the criminal and used that knowledge to maintain a ruthless control. For him, however, his overall lack of moral character would never allow him to keep a badge.

Doc Holliday of the Wyatt Earp fame was a notorious gam-bler and gunfighter – originally from the old South. Having

John Henry "Doc" Holliday

graduated dental school in Pennsylvania in 1872 at the age of 20, he returned to his native Georgia. His lung disease drove him west in search of drier climates. He eventually moved to the Southwest when he was diagnosed with tuberculosis at the ripe old age of 22. Holliday subsisted, battling his TB, his addictions to alcohol, gambling and women until his death at the age of 36. Legend is that he longed to have been a peace officer and he emulated his friend Wyatt Earp. No one understood better, perhaps the depravity of *the West*, than Doc. That insight might have made him an amazing sheriff.

Wyatt Earp

Wyatt Earp, the famed lawman, began his career as a constable in Lamar, Missouri in 1871. He was charged with mishandling funds and he took off before he could be arrested. Not long after, he was arrested for stealing horses. He could not pay the bail so he was jailed. He broke out of jail and headed west. Earp became known for his own code of justice. He lived his life according to that code of justice which can be summed up best as: 'what seemed right to him.' Political enemies of the Earps and friends of the Clantons tried to get Wyatt and his brothers for the death of Billy Clanton and two of the Mclaurys. The Earps shot them in a gunfight that was known then as the Fremont Street Fiasco. It was then that the Earps and Doc Holliday tried to disarm the Clantons and Mclaurys under the town ordinance of no firearms. Eventually officials ruled no charges were to be filed from the 30 second gunfight that has been built into lawman lore known as the

'Gunfight at the OK Corral'. Soon after, two of Wyatt's brothers were victims of persons seeking their own justice for the Clantons. Virgil was seriously hurt in an assassination attempt and his brother Morgan was murdered in retaliation for the *Freemont Street Fiasco*. Wyatt went on a ride of vengeance, reaping justice as only he could. His criminal instinct led him on his ride for vengeance justice and had he been able to maintain his standards along a civic line, he may have continued as a great peace officer. His brother, Virgil, though without the use of one arm did remain in law enforcement until his retirement and his reputation was unequaled.

The 'Old West' of America has become so much a mixture of lore and legend that it is sometimes difficult to remember that there were many amazing events happening around the world with rapid technological and political advancements being made while the 'West was being won.' New immigrants of almost every nation, as well as more and more Americans, were also making their way west to make their fame and fortune. Their adventures began certainly in full force prior to the California gold strike in 1849 and the driving of the last spike in the Transcontinental Railroad line at Promontory Point, Utah in May of 1869. The railway linked Council Bluffs, Missouri (across the river from Omaha, Nebraska) with the San Francisco Bay. It initiated a new speed of travel and a new era of crime.

 On July 21, 1873 outside of Adair, Iowa a little-known gang of thieves completed the first successful train robbery. The Rock Island Express was robbed; netting about $3,000 for the thieves. The soon to be infamous gang, calling themselves the James-Younger Gang, was led by Jesse James. James, who was just

26 years old at the time, had but a mere 8 years left prior to his death. Violence and theft were a part of the West that man could not seem to escape no matter how far he traveled. The greed that caused more deaths than can possibly be measured followed man wherever he went. At the most remote panning site for gold, along a creek with no name in distant Alaska, would likely be yet another miner murdered for his stake. Towns of the western territories had only the federal government's cavalry, governors of the territories, who were appointed and often corrupt, and circuit judges to help keep the peace. Often, the job of sheriff would, by necessity, go to the man with the fastest gun hand and the willingness to use it. It was inevitable that the line between criminals and lawmen would be so easily crossed. These men knew their towns and they maintained them as only one who had that local understanding could.

But changes were happening and as towns began to grow their ability toward self-governance would increase. Lawyers and educated men were moving west in hopes of finding adventure and a place to hang a shingle. The world outside the 'Old West' was traveling at break-neck speed as international trade was increasing and the speed of communication was enabling growth in national markets as well. The islands of Hawaii had completed trade agreements with the U.S. Suffrage movements were growing for former slaves and their progeny. Interestingly, the first black Congressman, Hiram Rhodes Revels, a Republican from Missouri was sworn into office on February 25, 1870. He was sworn in prior to African Americans being given the right to vote nationwide! The Fifteenth Amendment to the Constitution was ratified on March 30, 1870 guaranteeing nationally the right for non-white males to vote. In the presidential election of 1872, Susan B. Anthony cast an illegal vote to underscore women's suffrage. The push for women to have a say in government was being realized even in western towns. In the iconic film, "Rooster Cogburn," John Wayne plays opposite Kathryn Hepburn. As she bests him, in yet another verbal match of wits, Marshal Cogburn turns to the Indian boy 'Wolf' and says, "If they ever give them the vote… *Gawd help us!*" The movie is set in 1880. It would be another forty years before America would see the 19th Amendment ratified. American law enforcement outside of the West was beginning to understand these changes and that science was a new asset to criminal investigation.

AMERICAN LAW ENFORCEMENT COMES TO SCIENCE WITH THE WORLD

In Argentina, Juan Vucetich made the first criminal fingerprint identification in 1892. He identified Francisca Rojas, a woman who murdered her two sons and cut her own throat attempting to place blame on another. Her bloody print was left on a door post, proving her identity as the murderer.

Also in 1892, a British anthropologist, Sir Frances Galton enumerated the loops and whirls that were unique to fingerprints in his book. Those characteristics became known as the Galton Details. As early as 1883, famed American author Mark Twain wrote in his book *Life on the Mississippi* of a murderer being caught by use of his fingerprints! In 1896, the International Association of Chiefs of Police, headquartered in the U.S. (and still active) created the National Bureau of Criminal Identification for the exchange of information on crimes. In 1980, nearly one hundred years later *AFIS* the *Automated Fingerprint Identification System* became the first (and still vital) computer data base of fingerprint identifications. Policing in America was interconnected with the world while maintaining local law enforcement. The best balance for thwarting terrorists.

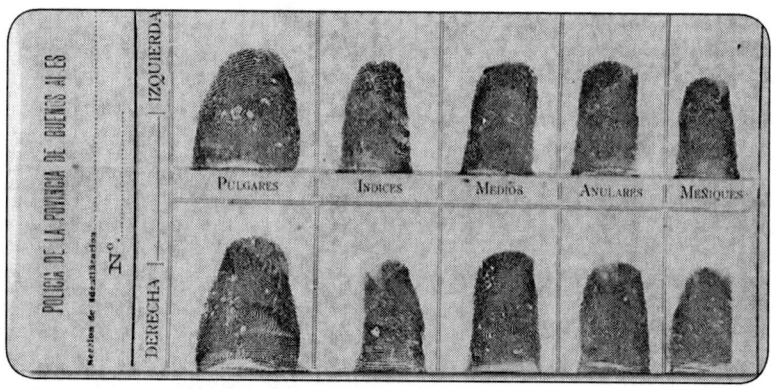

Francisca Roza's fingerprint card

Professional sports were also taking off in the areas of America's formerly rustic wilderness. The very first professional baseball game of the National Association was played April 4, 1871 between the Cleveland Forest Citys and the Fort Wayne, Indiana team the Kekiongas. For those, like the author who have lived all their lives in Northeast Ohio, it is good to know tradition holds across the centuries. In that first game, the final score was 2-0. Cleveland lost. This was the first time the immortal slogan of Cleveland sports fans was uttered, "There's always next year!"

Another American tradition is straight from the piers at Ellis Island, the ethnic, mostly poor, European populations for which early policing in cities like New York and Boston are famous. The St. Patrick's Day parades in these cities show-off some of that heritage of the local cops. A review of generations of cops through the first two centuries of law enforcement in America find a high percentage of Judeo-Christian beliefs represented. In many of the larger eastern cities cops of Roman Catholic heritage were a majority, with divisions between those of Italian versus Irish ancestry. It comes as a point of interest that one of the very first *terrorist groups* who operated in America were also from Irish descent. Operating ostensibly in the east coast region and involved in the coal mining strikes of the late 1800's was the *Molly Maguire's*. That group ended abruptly, so to speak, on June 21, 1877. The Irish terrorist society in the minefields surrounding Scranton, Pennsylvania was broken up when eleven leaders were hung for murders of police and mine officials.

Other early eastern U.S. city police officers were from an Orthodox faith interspersed with those who were from Protestant and Evangelical faiths. A much smaller number of Native Americans are found in some of the western regions, almost all as part of reservation police. Some of those brought with them their native faiths. What is not present are any generations in which law enforcement officers espousing the Muslim faith are in any great number. This lends support to the premise held by most American traditionalists that America is a country founded on the Judeo-Christian tenets as clearly seen in both the Declaration of Independence and the Constitution as well as the writings of many of the early founders of the country and its presidents.

The lack of a substantial number of Muslim law enforcement officers through the twentieth century in America has further widened the divide post 9-11 between the police and Islamic communities. The same low numbers of officers with faiths from eastern religions including Buddhism and Taoism or those of tribal descent, such as Animism or Spiritism, whether from the African Continent, South America or the Pacific Rim, would seem to support a similar schism between police and persons of these faiths. However, other than a heavy suspicion during WWII for those of the Japanese culture and a time of discord between those of Asian descent and law enforcement during and shortly after the Vietnam War, none have developed into the chasm that Islam and American law enforcement see between each other; primarily due in the early decades of the 21st century to the terrorist attacks pre-9-11; 9-11 itself and the ensuing wars.

The first decade of the 21st century became a time during which individuals and terrorist groups claiming the Islamic faith became the most visible enemy of America and for what she stands. Add to that vitriolic mix the fact that an increasing number of new police officers coming to the streets in that decade were veterans of the wars in the Middle East, it was a recipe for an '*us against them*' mentality. It is probable that every veteran from that era has a set of Iraqi Most Wanted Playing Cards, used by the military to keep the names and faces of wanted Iraqi's ever-present in the minds of the troops. Such a pre-conceived division between police and civilians has always existed to some degree. Americans, from their earliest colonial days, have what seems to be an innate distrust of government power and by association, those in government who visibly represent that power. It also stemmed from the belief by those in law enforcement that most civilians are unsupportive of the risks police take to protect those very same civilians. This was exacerbated in the 1960's and 70's when the schism between police and younger citizens particularly had grown to culture changing proportions. It is fair to say that both sides share in the perpetuation of this us against them mentality.

From the earliest days of policing in America, there was a precarious balance between good and evil; black and white and how much gray was there supposed to be in the mix. The result became that some officers saw themselves at odds with the civilian community or, sometimes, operated as though they were *above* that community. The days of graft and corruption in the days of *Serpico* in the NYPD painted many good cops with a very tainted brush. The pervasive attitudes though could extend to the point that the police felt their actions were above questioning. The dichotomy made the concept of police and citizens working together even less likely, even though, hindsight informs those who look that working together was exactly what was needed to prevent the terrorists who would soon infiltrate America's cities. Terrorist acts on American shores, however, were not on very many people's radar.

These earliest police on America's streets in places like New York City were a mixture of the well-educated and many poorly educated men, both simply trying to put food on the table for their families and provide a service to their new homelands. Corruption found fallow ground in which to grow; brought about in part by low pay and difficult work under a judicial system that was at times corrupt that blurred the black and white of the law into shades of gray. Such was the continuing struggle between the ideal and the world of the street officer. That is why, if a new design for law enforcement and Americans to be working hand in hand to stop the advancement of terrorism in our country is to be drawn, then it must be sketched with an understanding of who are *American Police.*

AMERICA'S POLICE VERSUS AMERICAN POLICE

Understanding this diverse and rugged background of policing in America's first century or so helps in understanding the dichotomy between *America's Police* and *American Police*. It is more than a matter of semantics. America's police, if defined by a common understanding of the language is a reference to the type of law enforcement the citizens of the United States are expecting when they have contact with them. It refers to the type of police that must be in place if the agencies are to enjoy any degree of community support. Conventional wisdom maintains a basic level of trust and acceptance of the role of local police is necessary if bond levies or other displays of public support which results in financial stability for the department are to be retained. The glaring problem with such a setup is simply, *which of the competing groups within a community gets to be the one to write the definition of common understanding?* The way in which the department is going to respond to the widest spectrum of a community's population cannot be blown about by changing winds of political correctness. There must be a standard of fairness, of professionalism, and a commitment to protecting those who are most vulnerable in society whether it is the aged or infirm, the children or the destitute as correctly as they would care for those of prestige and importance, wealth and power.

Perhaps the best and clearest example of the standard that is American Policing came from a man this author met mid-way through the first decade of the 21st century within just a few miles of the Russia Ukraine border before the days of Vladimir Putin's *non-invasion* of the Crimea. The man lay on small sofa bed on a sun porch, debilitated by pain from spinal disease. As I had considerable time to talk with him, eventually he asked what the logo was on the Bible I was holding. I explained it represented a police badge (the Bible was a "Police Officer's Bible" by Holman Publishers). I shared I was a retired American police officer. He then explained, through his interpreter that he was former KGB, (Soviet secret police). He went on to explain that shortly after the fall of Communism he had an opportunity to meet American police officers for the very first time. He said that was when he finally understood the difference. It came down to a simple dichotomy. American police, he said were there to protect. "We (the Russian police and the KGB)", were there to punish." The Komitet Gosudarstvennoy Bezopasnosti, (KGB) which is translated the Committee for the Security of the USSR model which existed from 1954 to 1991 in the United Soviet Socialist Republic resembles more the first known police in ancient Egypt about 3000 B.C. There the country was divided into 47 jurisdictions and the ruler of each area was "chief of police, who bore the title *sab heri seker*, or "chief of the hitters." All of this is not to say some less than professional forces have used American police to punish and persecute rather than protect and prosecute. But those are the exception and not the rule. From the earliest agencies, American police sought to be protectors.

These observations are made in completely different millennium than when the first police officers, some say like those working for the Pinkerton Detective Agency, were as diverse as the country in which they worked. Expanding ever westward, under the name the United States of America, the land itself in many ways reflected the internal dichotomy of our own badge carrying officers of the peace. It was, in fact, the badges first worn by these lawmen that reflect the Great Divide that separated peace officers in the East from lawmen in the West.

THE GREAT DIVIDE

The Boston Police Department boasts the very first municipal police agency in the U.S. A badge of theirs is shown here.

The year on the badge is 1854 and appears to be a historical replica of the badges worn in those days. Cruder badges were often the fare of this first agency. An example of a badge from about the same era but from the New York Police Department Office of the Chief can be seen here as more basic than the shiny brass. Even still, an officer working out of the 'Chief's Office' would not be sporting a street officer's badge. Here is a more realistic look at the street officer's badge. And if a town could not afford to send away to have a badge made specifically for them, they created one with what they had at hand, such as this hand stamped quarter dollar shows.

The more rustic the badge, the more indicative of the man that might be wearing it. Some cities found themselves in times 'out west' of great financial success and the town council would show off their prestige with the badges. Uniformed police were much more confined to the East coast and eventually the West coast leaving the Southwestern and plain states to remain less formal and more individualistic.

Photo courtesy of CVSflags.com

Once out West, the badges took on the character of the man behind them. Here are some examples of the gap that was widening between the cultured East coast and the ruffian West and of course, everything is bigger and better, they say, in Texas, as this badge for Texas State Police declares.

There could be no discussion of the lawmen of the U.S. West without the U.S. Marshals and the Texas Rangers. Their fame is so great that many their badges have been forged and are marketed under a variety of false claims that have just enough realistic appeal to catch the unaware buyer up in the scam. The Marshals and Rangers helped create the legacy that has continued into the present time as exemplars of efficient law enforcement under very difficult circumstances.

Even as the appeal for the lure of the 'Old West' and the *quick justice* that went with a six-shooter or a 'hanging judge' continues in the reflections of many; there are calls today for a return to a law that provided the defense for shooting a *bad guy*. The law is claimed to have been simply, "He needed killin'." That particular law is more urban legend than truth. However, in a case in Kentucky when the defense was the shooter felt he was under a continual and unending threat of death of extraordinary tension, the judge explained to the jury, "...before a jury should acquit they should be well satisfied that the killing was not the offspring of bad passion, but solely of a thorough and well-founded belief that it was necessary for security."

BRINGING IT HOME

What then is the true nature of this divide that seems to have matured lawmen and peace officers from our country's first century and created our 'protection of the people' rather than persecution of the people in its second? Is it as simple as that from the county Justice of the Peace to the highest barrister of the Supreme Court of the United States; America is a country of free and brave citizens who have chosen to live out their lives under the Stars and Stripes, committed to the proposition that under the law, all men are equal in their standing. Every citizen has certain rights and responsibilities both go into a courtroom before a blind Lady Justice and it is she who is there to weigh out the facts. The judgment that is rendered is to be based only on the facts and not on the wealth, prestige or personage of the defendant.

Today, where there appears the division between those wearing a badge from one part of the country to another it is but a mirage, an optical illusion likely perpetrated by those outside of the world of law enforcement. It is simply not true. A line officer in the far flung reaches of the 49th state to the inner-city of any of the original 13 states will lay their lives on the line for one another, for each other's families and will travel incredible distances to honor the fallen among their brothers or sisters. Jesus once said, "Greater love has no one than this, than to lay down one's life for his friends"

There is no truer statement anywhere and perhaps no finer mortal example than those who hold taut the thin blue line. There comes an occasion in every great society across the annals of time, where that society must take stock of itself, particularly in those who held the reins of peace to decide whether or not those persons deserve to hold those reins. An iconic statement made from less than an iconic platform, declares "real peace is not just the absence of conflict but the presence of justice." Only those who truly understand this concept are fit to hold the society's reins of trust. Few, however, that are far removed from the average working citizen can grasp such a concept. The farther one resides from the commonality of his American brothers and sisters the more justice is defined by rank and privilege, power and prestige.

RE-DEFINING POLICE IN AMERICA

In the not so distant past, a new bureaucracy appeared on the American stage. Born out of crisis it became a living breathing organism all its own and seemed as if it would consume all those other agencies, departments, offices, officers, sheriffs, chiefs of police, deputies, marshals and the like whose shadow it fell across. At the time of this writing, the behemoth continues to breathe its fiery breath but its shadow does not cast as far as it once did. It seems to have begun the process of devouring itself by its own gluttony. By its own actions it brought itself into the scope of those agencies that it sought to overwhelm and now, their guard up; they will not be taken easily if, at all. The Department of Homeland Security soon became known for buying up billions of rounds of ammunition, bringing store shelves to near zero levels and causing average citizens to stand up and take notice. Then appeared the "DHS POLICE" vehicles on city streets and open highways, an armed federal agency without police powers that yet donned the police moniker. But it was not to stop there, no this seemingly out of control beast was about to overwhelm the population with its sheer size. An interesting thing, however, about Americans, as was learned in a previous section, they have a healthy distrust of government, particularly government that is centralized and at the federal level where it appears as if it is over all others and beyond the reach of the citizens. It was such a cry of foul that caused the citizens to revolt at the quartering of British troops in colonial homes, where the Red Coats knew no limits to their avarice. Americans are a strange breed. As much as some things must be carried out for sake of expedience and efficacy at the federal level – and as effective as the agents of the Federal Bureau of Investigation can be – local police and local citizenry keep a healthy distrust of such agencies. This author respects many very fine agents and belongs to one of the finest law enforcement associations ever established consisting of graduates of the FBI's National Academy; but the minute the *we are the* '___ insert federal alphabet soup lettering___' *and we are in charge* card is played, local law enforcement and the citizens they serve on a daily basis will be on their hind legs in a heartbeat. The adage of "hell hath no fury…" may well be true for a woman scorned; but a local citizenry deprived of their local control of their police and safety are running a close second to that disparaged damsel!

One thing the DHS's extreme over-stepping of their legislated authority has done, it has helped the FBI, the US Marshals, the Border Patrol and a host of other very legitimate and worthwhile federal agencies to be seen in a much better light by local cops all across the country for one main reason – they were *not* DHS. Upon the heels of the debacle of DHS wanna-be's running around playing policemen, word got out that almost every possible branch of the federal government had scripted some kind of a police or enforcement body for their very own. Some are beyond laughable to the point of near insanity. There is the *U.S. Mint Police*, though no one seems to know if that is where they serve or how they taste. The next time you are fed up with law enforcement and you shout, *those damn police!* You may actually get a call from the *U. S. Bureau of Reclamation Dam Police!* The smallest federal police agency is the *U.S. Supreme Court Police*. And it is possible to go on and on but it has become apparent almost every single federal agency feels the need to have their very own police powers ready at hand. One last quirk, although there are hundreds that could be mentioned, if one considers all that ammunition that has been bought up by the Feds… the *U.S. Department of Veterans Affairs Police*, which has a separate Chief of the USDVAP for each Veteran's Hospital where they serve, is probably not responsible for the shortage of ammo. From 1973, when they became federal police, until 1999 they weren't allowed guns. They were only issued those just before the turn of this 21st century! With 2.2 Billion rounds of ammunition bought by the federal government recently, over 1.8 billion going just to DHS, it is good to know the *U.S. Postal Inspectors* got a large chunk of ammunition as well. You wouldn't want those delivering all that ammunition to not have some of their own, would you? Then, of course, there was plenty for the *Environmental Protection Agency.* Apparently, the EPA needed a great deal of deadly force for their *SWAT* team. Yes, the EPA has its own SWAT team. Someone thought that perhaps it was an acronym for Scientists with Army Toys. In any event, America has come to the point where it needs to reflect on who is holding the reins for the peace and protection of the citizens

If history is a lesson then pay close attention because the best holder of the reins is the one who must ride the horse. In this case, as in most societies, it is the citizen or the local constable who is closest to those citizens and is one of them. It is their own arse up in the saddle and they have more common sense than most about how their horse takes to the bit.

CITIZEN SOLDIERS/CITIZEN COPS

It was early spring, 1975. The Vietnam War was winding to a close but not the way anyone in our family had expected it would. All these years later the debate continues about what or who lost the war for us. Some will claim it was Eisenhower or Kennedy for getting us involved where the French had been annihilated for over a decade. Some swear it was Johnson's guns and butter programs of the 1960's, his waffling due to political pressure that turned the tide of the war against the United States while others blame Nixon for being too concerned with winning re-election and his détente with the Chinese.

It was about this time I entered the U.S. Air Force Reserve. For those readers who know only about the Reserve and National Guard forces from the 1990's through the first decade of this century, it may be difficult to comprehend what is about to be described. The reason is simple. These last two and a half decades have been a proving ground, a crucible of fire for these citizen soldiers and they have proven themselves well. Such was *not* the case in 1975. The men I served with in our Weapons System Security Flight had seen combat while assigned as Active Duty but not since they had joined the Reserves. Because of that the deployment plans for the Reserve unit to which I was assigned was to replace an Active Duty force on their home base while the *real soldiers* went to war. I believe this was common practice at least across 10th Air Force. Reserve/Guard units were always separate from the *real soldiers.* Never would you see one embedded with the other. A great example was our assignment. We were to go to from our unit in NE Ohio to a base in the South. Those units would deploy and we would take over the functions as the *B Team* while they went to war. Remember I was part of a Weapons System Security Flight. Our role was to protect priority A, B, and C weapons systems. The base to which we were assigned did not have *any* priority weapons systems of any kind. Our unit might deploy but we would have absolutely no function once we got there. Which was good because we had not had any hands-on training and, for the most part, we did not have any of the correct equipment other than some antiquated .38 revolvers and M-16 rifles. Those who had handcuffs for securing an intruder on the flight line had brought their own (most of us were civilian cops). What training or skills we had, we brought with us. At our own base, we were given whatever corner of whatever building no one else wanted during those early years.

Training at the Basic Military Training Squadron at Lackland AFB was the only time that Regulars, National Guard and Reserves were embedded in the same flights. A good start *if you have the right kind of trainer.* If the trainer is one who, as with our original T.I. (Training Instructor) was most likely suffering from severe PTSD (although no one would have diagnosed nor treated in 1975), who saw all those who were not *regulars* as interlopers who were, in his words: "Only there to f*** with the morale of his regulars" it will not be a worthwhile training experience. Remember, I mentioned these were the same months when Saigon fell and our troops were headed home but not to parades and ticker-tape rather to bottles filled with human urine and horrific names being thrown at them.

The police trainers that are chosen to train these new civilian counterparts described in the following chapters must be very much in agreement with the concept. If you assign them a trainer who literally despises them for being civilians instead of cops; then you better have civilians who will not bolt for the door the first time the trainer tears apart a metal desk or bedframe and throws it at them (true story). That example is a bit strong but the trainers' attitudes toward the recruits will be easily felt. Do not look for the warm and cuddly type, either. We are not sending these new persons out to teach D.A.R.E. classes to first graders; we are training them to be another set of eyes with the cops; to know how to battle terrorists together. When our flight got a new T.I we excelled. Previously we were beginning to look like Bill Murray's unit in Columbia Pictures' *Stripes.*

That has all changed I am pleased to say but it gives us a great analogy for how *not* to integrate a new Civilian Centurion Corps into our blue ranks and spend decades making the same mistakes.

Headquarters and Security Police Squadron, YMA, Vienna OH

With al Qaeda and ISIS at our doorsteps and 'coming to a town or county near you' soon; it is time to take a few pages from those old police training lessons and re-write them for the Centurions of today and tomorrow. Not everything was poorly done or outdated. There were some quality concepts. The first two principles that must be adopted are not so much an <u>add-on</u> to what we do but rather in a genetic sense as part of our <u>cultural DNA</u> as who we are. Simply stated:

1. We are the first line of defense against any and all who would seek to take from us those God-given and inalienable rights which are constitutionally protected. As a community of Americans, we will strive together to protect every person among us from all enemies foreign and domestic; the stron-

gest to the weakest, the richest to the poorest, and the natural born citizen to the legal immigrant desiring citizenship.

2. We commit together that our security begins within each home and the sanctity of those homes. The strength each requires is resolute and shall not be diminished by any act of law which demeans the roles of father and mother; their right to worship, to exercise their faith in any way which presents no harm to others and to raise their children according to that faith without interference. These shall always remain foundational to our community.

It is the genetic design of these two principles which will enable the *new centurions* to step forward together in solidarity to protect their communities. The centurions described here are not isolationists within their specific community, rather they understand each community is an integral part of the whole. It is all the communities together that make America. Without all the states, America could not be *The United States* through which we find, in part, our identity in the world and our combined strength is far superior to the individual parts of the whole.

It is within this new *DNA* local law enforcement professionals can *stretch the thin blue line* to include those who are not full-time cops but rather are *citizen cops* as the militia of colonial times or the military Reserve and National Guard of today. From the current make-up of our country's National Guard and Reserves is a crucial lesson in what makes the *citizen soldier* concept work so effectively. Many of these soldiers are performing identical or similar functions in their civilian lives as they perform in their military ones. Certainly, there are some who are business executives during the week and fighter pilots on the weekend but both are leaders. Many, however, are performing the same kind of technical jobs in the civilian world whether it is information system technology, logistics, firefighting, records, analysis or routine vehicle maintenance, the skills they have honed during their daily lives are used to the group's advantage in their respective military units. The concept of bringing local citizens into the world of policing it does not automatically require every single citizen is going to don a badge and a gun and *go shoot the bad guys.*

Everyone will be capable to utilize a weapon, just as in the military but that may not be their primary assignment. In the movie, *The Battle of the Bulge,* the German forces are overwhelming Bastogne and a half dozen other cities along a sparse American held line. As the American and other Allied forces are hurriedly *advancing to the rear* – a colonel walks in on a group of cooks and asks where their weapons are. They reply they are cooks. He informs them that "You're in the infantry now – get a rifle." The new *thin blue line* will make excellent use of the non-fighting skills of the *new centurions* but each must be aware that when push comes to shove, they are all *in the infantry.* Just as those soldiers, the cooks who were stationed at Bastogne did not have to go seek out and engage the enemy because the enemy was coming quickly upon them; the new centurions of today need not look very far because the world is bringing the danger to our very doorsteps.

Chapter 2

The World At Our Doorstep

Invasion I.T.

The *Information Age* is a time when the 'Millennials' are able to have it *their way.* Just before the turn of the century during an interview with CNN's Wolf Blitzer, (March 9, 1999), then Vice President Al Gore answered the question as to what made him different than the other candidates for the Presidency. He replied, "During my service in the United States Congress, I took the initiative in creating the Internet."

Snopes, in their own way, was quick to explain what the Vice President *meant* to say and it wasn't that he really invented the technical aspects of the internet; but it was what he did in Congress that made it possible for the internet to exist. Whether what Mr. Gore did in Congress was essential for the internet to come into existence will be judged by history. His reputation is as one who can have an inflated view as to the importance of his own work. History can be the judge but as for the importance of the internet in daily lives, you need to only turn on the television, go to pay a bill or buy a gallon of milk. Every aspect of our daily lives is, in some way, touched by the internet.

One can imagine what today's world would be like without the internet, the microfibers and memory chips. If Shakespeare lived in this century, perhaps Romeo and Juliet would have texted each other and saved their own lives! The vast majority of everything internet related can trace their origin to the technical inventions of Israel over the last several decades. Just a glance at http://www.israel21c.org/technology/israels-top-45-greatest-inventions-of-all-time-2/ will provide a hint as to the source for much of what is the inter-connected world of the internet. It is, however, that same inter-connectedness that brings not only to our doorsteps but into our homes one of the greatest threats to our way of life. Dependence upon the technology behind all of the wonderful time saving, communication and data transmission apps has created an Achilles' heel for our entire society that could cost us our existence.

KnowYour Enemy is a saying derived from Sun Tzu's *The Art of War* and there have been few lessons for survival in war time that are more critical than this. This poster from World War II is one of hundreds that were used to help the civilians who were not fighting overseas but rather were needed stateside to keep the factories running, the *victory gardens* growing, metal and rubber products being recycled and, most importantly, the families intact. It was the 'family back home' for which the soldiers were fighting. If that crumbled so would the soldiers' fighting spirit, the will to slog on through the mud and in the cold against horrendous odds. The drive to win would all but disappear. It was critical for victory that the civilians at home stand shoulder to shoulder with those serving in the Armed Forces.

A second inspiration of the fight for total victory in World War II was a understanding between the men and women who were fighting that a stanza from a WWI inspirational song titled, "Over There" The lyric was simply, "…and we won't come back 'til it's over, over there." The fighting forces of the Second World War understood like those of the First that they were in it for the long haul. The only way these men knew they could get home other than in a flag draped box or on a hospital ship was to survive the entire deal and win! There were other rough methodologies, the number of points awarded for specific amount of action seen but the truth of the matter was the only sure way was to have a Victory in Europe (VE) day and then a Victory over Japan (VJ) day. Even once there was victory in Europe, many of those troops were reassigned to the Pacific theater of operations to continue to fight until the war against all the Axis powers was complete. Modern wars from the time of Vietnam forward have done away with this methodology which had been used since at a minimum the destruction of Carthage by the Romans between 149 and 146 BC. It is now considered obsolete and not good for the general welfare of the troops. There are some who might argue that the Vietnam era's 360 days and a wake-up and what that meant to the war effort overall and the final outcome of the Vietnam war may have been more deleterious to the overall mental health of hundreds of thousands of vets more so than the other. Time and historians will be the better judge of that question. The same is true for the seemingly countless deployments to the Middle East theater for many over-used units and their families.

In the war against terrorists every single citizen of the United States had better learn new lyrics to that WWI song. Perhaps the lyrics might be, *"They are here. They are here. Send the word, send the word they are here! We're going to fight them. We're going to fight them and we won't stop fighting until we drive them out of here!"* In this war, the one that is now and will continue to be fought in foreign theaters as well as on our home soil, there will be no 360 days and a wake up, no rotation points and no hardship leave particularly if Iran succeeds in getting the nuclear arsenal they so strongly desire. This might be the only *recruitment poster* for this war...

A SOMBER MESSAGE?

Yes, it most certainly is but it is a realistic one and one to which the citizens of this great nation must ascribe if the U.S.A. is going to come through it better than the Carthaginians did in 164 BC when every last evidence of that dramatic city which was once Carthage was scattered to the sands of Tunisia.

It is at this point perhaps a word needs to be added concerning the critical need for persons within the community, both on the police departments and within the local citizenry to develop a foundation of trust for one another before the *stretching* of the *thin blue line* can truly begin. It has been discussed so far in this text how the police officer came to be in the United States and how the profession has continued to develop and grow in its capabilities, its roles and the demands placed upon it by communities. But little has been said about the commonalities between the police and the community can make for the foundation of trust that is so vital.

When soldiers stand shoulder to shoulder with one another in the heat of battle, they are often exhausted, hungry, scared and in many ways completely different than the soldier with whom they are paired. Off the battlefield, without the common ground of training, the common experiences and frustrations, the common losses and the common victories, they may never have even chosen to speak with one another. But, once they did have those common experiences and more importantly, they share common goals: their survival, the survival of their squad and victory for their nation they can form an inseparable bond.

To build elasticity into the *thin blue line* that will accept those from within the community who seek to help as well as make the line a place where people from the community would choose to be, there must be a ***foundation of mutual commonalities***. It is important, perhaps at this point, to concede there are some who will never chose to stand with local law enforcement to fend off the predators who seek to devour and destroy our society. Their reasons will fill volumes mostly with tired old adages. Their excuses and bigotry will keep them from allowing their red blood of humanity to be matched with the blue from which the line is formed. They may claim a distrust of the *system* or some other worn-out line but it comes down to their own refusal to see with open eyes, to hear with open ears and to trust with an open heart.

The events in Ferguson Missouri between August and December of 2014 are testimony to such simple mindedness. Even as the prosecutor outlined all of the exceptional and exemplary precautions he took to insure the grand jury had every piece of evidence with which to make their decision; there were many in the racially charged atmosphere that had their own minds made up and they did not wish to be disturbed with the facts. They believed the white officer murdered the unarmed black teenager and no amount of testimony will change their minds. Those types of folks will never seek to be part of this solution. They will, however, find that by not being part of the solution, they will be prey to those who seek to devour. They and their young people, their children, their aged and infirm will be the first of those who find themselves destroyed by the forces that come against the community. Just as wild animals while hunting seek to separate the strong and fast of the herd from the weak and slow to make for an easier, quicker kill of the less capable; those of the terrorist groups such as ISIS and al Qaida will seek to exploit such foolishness and will soon cut their prey from the community herd and attempt to fill themselves on the spoils they have garnered by their attack. It is imperative to not waste time bemoaning those who refuse to come along, who spew hatred and ignorance as if the rest of society cannot survive without them or to carry a guilt there should be something more that could have been done to help them see. The ability to let it go comes from understanding it is their choice. That is where it must be left because for the rest of the clan there is much work to be done.

How is a *foundation of mutual commonalities* built? It serves this purpose well to take a page from the military methodologies of *boot camp*. There are several objectives the instructors of new military recruits (those who *push boots*) have for the recruits to learn prior to the conclusion of the basic training period. These objectives involve learning basic military courtesy, military history, basic marksmanship and a dozen other basic building blocks for them to have prior to their next level of training. There is one primary goal that over arches each of these objectives. The instructor seeks to transform that recruit from an "I" to a "we". There is methodology to everyone dressing alike with the same haircut, the same sleeping quarters, the same layout of the foot locker. The 'individual' must become lost in the 'we'. Part of the methodology is to remove all the individualistic styles and trappings and reduce them to their lowest common denominator. Later in their military career they can choose whether to have boxers or briefs but initially, even that is not a matter for individual selection. You learn to act as one, move as one, think as one and *listen* as one. To bring such a divergent group together into a single unit requires the individual going through the transformation has the motivation to comply.

In the 1967 WWII movie with Lee Marvin as Major Riesman, *The Dirty Dozen* has a plot where the major must transform twelve U.S. Army prisoners, all convicted of various crimes against the army or the civilian population into a crack fighting unit to go behind enemy lines and do their deeds *for* the army. Most of the twelve are scheduled to be hanged for their misdeeds. It was critical for the major to find the motivation that would apply to every one of the convicts. Major Riesman found just the right mix. "There will be no excuse, no appeal. Any attempt *by one of you* (to escape) and *you will all* be sent directly back to prison for execution of sentence. *You are therefore dependent upon each other.* Any one of you try anything smart, and all get it right in the neck.

Am I clear?" The major had found a very solid motivational tool but it still is based on a negative which can backfire.

The situation with ISIS and the threats that lone ranger jihadists will do these same horrific things within the homelands of the American people, that in and of itself can be very motivational. When the threats of what *might happen* become news reports of what *is happening;* those reports can be immensely motivating. News of these events happening on the other side of the world does not have the same impact, if it has any at all. It is when it is in *your town*, in *your neighborhood* and then *on your doorstep* the motivation becomes real. But by then, it is too late to prepare. Seek to know ahead of the invasion what the enemy has in store so that you can be ready when they are on your doorstep. Then you will be prepared to answer that door as was described at the beginning, to meet them face to face and, to take a line from John Wayne as Lt. Col. Benjamin Vandervoort in the 1962 WWII movie *The Longest Day*, "You can't give the enemy a break. Send him to hell."

One need not look long for news stories that are developing rapidly on the threat that is currently held like the Sword of Damocles over the United States. Authorities are screaming warnings about the vulnerability of the infrastructure upholding our power grids across the U.S. Cascade failures are possible with the slightest infiltration at key sites along the system which could cripple large sections of the country. In many places, it would not even require infiltration, but a well-placed sniper's shot on certain of these power stations would have just as devastating an effect. Previously, coddlers in Washington sought to assuage the public fear by speaking of redundancy of systems that would prohibit a system wide shut-down; but, experience has shown that a protective system is a pipe dream.

Sources indicate that persons who have the position to be aware of threats to the United States' power sources have stated, for public record, *a single cyber-attack could shut down the entire U.S. power grid.* "Speaking at a House Intelligence Commute hearing, Admiral Michael Rogers, director of the National Security Agency and commander of the U.S. Cyber Command, admitted that China, and a handful of other countries currently possess the power to launch a cyber-attack that would shut down the entire U.S. power grid. At the hearing, Rogers said U.S. adversaries are performing electronic "reconnaissance" on a regular basis so that they can be in a position to disrupt the industrial control systems that run everything from chemical facilities to water treatment plants." In further testimony, Admiral Rogers stated unequivocally, "China and 'probably one or two' other countries have the ability to invade and possibly shut down computer systems of U.S. power utilities, aviation networks and financial companies…"

Shortly after the terrorist attacks on 9-11, when I had been retired for only three years, I was chomping at the bit to do something useful. But what? As I stood outside my home with my dogs, a man I had met a few times while I was chief of police drove into my drive. He was in a nearly brand new jeep painted the same yellow and black colors of Ohio sheriffs' vehicles and it sported a new logo on the side that said something to the effect of *homeland security.* He informed me he had connected with a group out of D.C. with the purpose to organize groups of citizens, like me, who longed to be part of a solution. The goal was to recreate the old Civil Defense Corps with one clear focus, the guarding of local power plants and electrical sub-stations. *Not the most glamourous job on the planet* and in 2001 there seemed to be little need for such a guard post. As you might imagine, his recruiting efforts did not go far. Without a sense of urgency, a purpose that is valued, and a leader who can motivate and inspire as well as explain the purpose of the mission, recruitment will be all up hill.

At this point, it is apparent an invasion has begun. The initial probing by covert sources gathering HUMINTT or human intelligence about America's weak spots is on-going. There are cyber-probes happening continually and man-made interruptions in the nation's power-grids and within the information networks this country runs on are searching for just the right combination to take down the system. In the cyber world, there are clear attempts to use the information gained to disrupt the ability of America's own covert operatives to maintain their secret identities. All the pre-invasion tactics are being used and those who are trained to recognize the indicators of a pending invasion are raising the clarion call; but, in Washington the call is landing on deaf ears. It must not be that the same thing will happen with the vast majority of the American populace. The fact that the invasion may not be a *hot war* with guns blazing and troop ships landing off the coast of North Carolina will make it more difficult for many to understand the inherent danger.

Many will see the drama played out along the U.S. and Mexico border as just an issue of people coming that are a problem for our communities from the point of resources, jobs and the issue of their illegal status. However, just as a rapist or thief may stand outside a locked door to a college dorm and pretend he is searching for his card to swipe it and gain entry waiting for a group of students who will come by and in their politeness even hold the door open for him; jihadists, drug dealers of the worst kind, spies, and deadly operatives will come sailing across our southern border and our extremely porous northern border with ease. All the while, certain political factions in Washington will be claiming we are discriminating against these folks because they are poor and we should be welcoming all of them with open arms. There is a Trojan horse sitting at our borders and we are opening wide the gates to bring it in.

The danger is not always from the outside, however. Perhaps the greatest threat to America in these foreboding times comes not from across a border or through the air in cyber-space but is within our own homes. It is time that, as we prepare to strengthen the fabric of the thin blue line we must also strengthen the moral fiber of our nation by paying close attention to the needs within families. The greatest battle that will be waged for America's future has already begun and it is within our own homes.

THE BATTLE FOR OUR HOMES

Missing in Action

The horrors of war know no bounds. During the Vietnam War, members of the 1st Cavalry were facing some incredibly vicious fighting against the Viet Cong in some of the bloodiest battles of the early years for America in the war. Telegrams were sent by Western Union to notify the wives of the news and there were so many each day the number of them was mind-numbing. The carriers were faced with an overwhelming task. Normally such messages were delivered along with some consoling at least from an officer and perhaps a chaplain from the military. It was tragic to receive word of a son or husband who was KIA, killed in action. It was mind numbing to get word that a loved one was taken as a POW, prisoner of war. Perhaps, though, as hard as those messages were to receive, the worst must have been that their spouse or child was MIA, missing in action. Sometimes, years would go on until it was resolved and some, even fifty years later have no idea whatever happened to their loved one.

As horrific as that must have been for those families, there are families today that have the same awful fact to deal with, their spouse, the father of the children and the one person who is supposed to be the biblical authority of the home has *chosen* to go MIA. He has not been taken prisoner by some foreign fighting force and never reported; he has not been killed but his body not recovered from some hell of a battle scene. No, this father, this spouse has decided to just leave; walk away from all his God-mandated responsibilities. Statistics tell us 1 out of every 3 children are without a father (also a mother but to a less degree), not by death but by choice. Of thousands upon thousands of men who get married every year in the U.S., another number that is rising is the number of divorces. A recent report by Mail On-Line reported that the current marriage and divorce rates in the U.S. are:

- Marriage rate: 6.8 per 1,000 total population
- Divorce rate: 3.6 per 1,000 population (44 reporting States and D.C.)

As difficult as that is; there are thousands more who never bothered with marriage and have chosen to just walk away when a baby came along or things got a little more difficult than they preferred. In America, the fatherless home is an epidemic. Nation-wide the statistics are unbelievable. The number of two-parent households fell by 1.2 million. Few ever come back. Fewer still live up to any obligations to their children. The real sadness comes from how those homes perpetuate more homes just like them. De-cades of absentee fathers have produced subsequent generations of the same. "Children living in single-parent and/or low-income households are more likely to exhibit problem behaviors and de-pressive symptoms and are less likely to display social competence than are children who grow up in more fortunate circumstances. The most common problems seen in single parent family's chil-dren are depression, stress, loneliness, aggression, compliance, smoke, alcohol, (and) narcotics. Children of single parents still have increased risks of mortality severe morbidity, and injury."

A recent NY Times article reported, "Studies also now indicate that about one-third of people who are abused in childhood will become abusers themselves. This is a lower percentage than many experts had expected, but obviously poses a major social challenge. The research also confirms that abuse in childhood increases the likelihood in adulthood of problems ranging from depression and alcoholism to sexual maladjustment and multiple personality.".

Rest assured, this is not just in Black America it is entire genera-tions of multiple cultures. The impact this has on our nation's and our communities' security is overwhelming. The following chart shows the loss of two parent households.

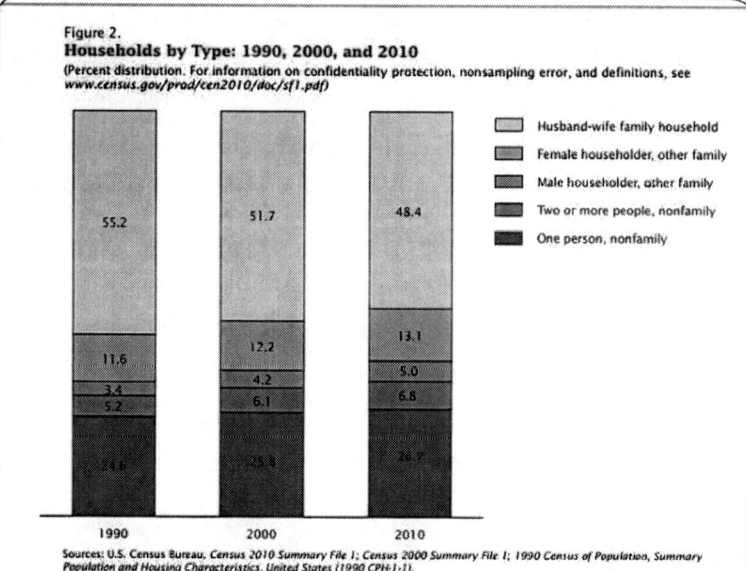

Figure 2.
Households by Type: 1990, 2000, and 2010
(Percent distribution. For information on confidentiality protection, nonsampling error, and definitions, see www.census.gov/prod/cen2010/doc/sf1.pdf)

Legend:
- Husband-wife family household
- Female householder, other family
- Male householder, other family
- Two or more people, nonfamily
- One person, nonfamily

Sources: U.S. Census Bureau, Census 2010 Summary File 1; Census 2000 Summary File 1; 1990 Census of Population, Summary Population and Housing Characteristics, United States (1990 CPH-1-1).

Children In Single-parent Families By Race

Year(s): 5 selected | Race: All | Data Type: All

Data Provided by: National KIDS COUNT

Location	Race	Data Type	2008	2009	2010	2011	2012
United States	American Indian	Number	308,000	334,000	350,000	355,000	345,000
		Percent	50%	53%	52%	53%	53%
	Asian or Pacific Islander	Number	467,000	508,000	539,000	559,000	579,000
		Percent	16%	16%	16%	17%	17%
	Black or African American	Number	6,195,000	6,471,000	6,533,000	6,509,000	6,493,000
		Percent	65%	67%	66%	67%	67%
	Hispanic or Latino	Number	5,731,000	6,322,000	6,674,000	6,890,000	7,008,000
		Percent	38%	40%	41%	42%	42%
	Non-Hispanic White	Number	9,193,000	9,406,000	9,329,000	9,466,000	9,358,000
		Percent	23%	24%	24%	25%	25%
	Total	Number	22,659,000	23,808,000	24,297,000	24,718,000	24,725,000
		Percent	32%	34%	34%	35%	35%
	Two or More Races	Number	1,319,000	1,411,000	1,586,000	1,655,000	1,703,000
		Percent	41%	41%	42%	42%	43%

Additional statistics over the last five years indicate a disturbing trend. The chart from the Kids Count Data Center points out the facts that should concern all American citizens.

The chart shows an unyielding set of stats that highlight distressing figures for several different races in our nation but it is particularly distressing for *Black Americans. American Indian* and *Hispanic or Latino* and *Two or More Mixed Races* have consistently difficult numbers. Above sixty-five percent, fifty percent, above forty percent (last four of five years) and above forty percent respectively of families with single parents. Social consequences loom darkly over many from such homes.

Persons who are disaffected socially, as brought out in the study reported in the NY Times article previously, have been empirically recognized as recruits for gangs across the U.S. and elsewhere. That is expanding as the need for terrorist foot-soldiers increases. In a recent NYU study on terrorist recruitment, results indicated, "despite their educational and financial background, (recruits) will feel alienated from society. It is this disenfranchised segment of the population that will be more susceptible to recruitment… For the disenfranchised that feel displaced from society or who want to act but are not able to act individually, the terrorist group provides that justification for action that recruits may need."
World-wide, terror cells are reaching out to find appropriate recruits for their causes. Recruiting tactics have expanded greatly as Islamic terrorist organizations have found fertile recruiting grounds in the Western hemisphere."

The question becomes, how can police and local communities *stretch the thin blue line* in a way that will offset the consequences of these single parent, and mostly fatherless, homes? Whether those disaffected socially by their lack of parental involvement turn to terrorist cells for self-actualization or remain a loner, drug or alcohol abuser and thereby a non-productive member of a local community, there remains a possibility that by reaching beyond problems to the individuals and including them for their skills as part of something bigger than themselves, the thin blue line may be a positive motivation.

Is it possible the systemic family issues in our nation which help to fuel the distrust between races, between certain members of all races including those who are on the low end of the single-family numbers such as the Asian and Pacific Islander as well as many in the non-Hispanic White communities can be in some part mitigated by inclusion in the Blue Line under a common cause which would open communication and possibly even understanding? This is no panacea soft-soap sell that with a few hugs and choruses of *Kumbaya* all the issues of society will be cured. As was stated clearly earlier, there will always be those who refuse to trust, to refuse to become involved in the solution and for those people when the very real threats against our nation are in our towns and upon our city streets; those same people will be possibly left outside the protection, the solution that the line has provided.

KEEPING THE FAITH

For a great many years, police officers in America who are of the Catholic faith wore a St. Michael medal understanding Michael the Archangel as being the patron saint and protector of Police Officers as well as many in military service, specifically the Airborne Infantry. An interesting side note, in the movie *The Untouchables,* when Elliot Ness asks Malone (Connery) what it was on his chain, Malone replies, "Ah, I'm with a heathen!" He goes on to identify his call box key and his medal of St. Jude. George Stone interrupts and explains he is the "Patron Saint of Lost Causes" (which is correct) but Malone adds, "and Policemen" (which is incorrect but better for the storyline than strong, avenging Michael the Archangel).

While I was Chief of Police I was regularly attending church where I taught Bible classes but on one Sunday I was to speak at a nearby church for Government Appreciation Day. The pastor introduced me and then added, "I did not know that it was possible to be a policeman and a Christian." I nearly hit the floor. I think my jaw did. There was a second similar occurrence having met a man who was an evangelist who was to speak at the television station our town, I took him to the television station so he could find his way. Not having been there before I introduced myself to the young lady at the first counter and she replied, somewhat amazed, "I didn't know a policeman could be a Christian!" Was it possible police officers nationwide are thought of as godless in the 1990's or was it just *my* department that was leaving such an image? Since both persons who made the comment did not live in *my* city, I assumed it was a larger difficulty and one, I believe, we have brought upon ourselves. It is one we must change if we are going to successfully *stretch the thin blue line.*

James, the brother of Christ and the first century head of the church in Jerusalem but who had not been an Apostle, wrote an incredibly common sense appreciation for faith.

"What *does it* profit, my brethren, if someone says he has faith but does not have works? Can faith save him? If a brother or sister is naked and destitute of daily food, and one of you says to them, "Depart in peace, be warmed and filled," but you do not give them the things which are needed for the body, what *does it* profit? Thus also faith by itself, if it does not have works, is dead. But someone will say, "You have faith, and I have works." Show me your faith without your works, and I will show you my faith by my works."

James was not claiming Paul was wrong when saying salvation is by faith alone. What he was saying was to those who claimed to have faith but did not show it by their actions that: true faith shows its love for God in a manner that matters. For anyone who has fallen in love, particularly those who have been married for some time, when there are no loving actions toward your spouse, he or she may begin to doubt the sincerity of your love. It is natural, at least early in relationships that when you truly love someone; you desire to find ways to show that love. How should police officers who are Christian show their faith, to their brothers in the line and to the public they serve? Are their legal decisions from liberal courts that have handcuffed the police in this area?

I will answer the latter question first. The answer is no. There are limitations for officers and departments using the authority of their offices and the symbol of that authority, the badge to require persons to listen to a testimonial or presentation of the Gospel message. But there is much you can do and it is time we make a list of things we *are not legally restricted from doing*.

Keeping the faith must first begin with the individual officer or civilian employee. My wife, who is a physician, often explains to her patients, especially moms, that if they do not take care of themselves, they will not be able to take care of anyone else. The same is true in our spiritual walk. Unless we are men and women of The Book (a term used for early Christians) then we will not be prepared for what God has in store for us each day in the ministry He has given us as police officers. Did you catch what I called your work? A ministry. When you believe your work and your life is a ministry that is Christ working through YOU! You are His hands and feet here on earth. That does not prevent you from arresting someone or using force against someone. Paul wrote in his letter to the Romans that: "For the one in authority is God's servant for your good. But if you do wrong, be afraid, for rulers do not bear the sword for no reason. They are God's servants, agents of wrath to bring punishment on the wrongdoer." This, of course, does not make the police officer the cop judge, jury and executioner but it does show the cop is the one to bring that evil to justice.

Where do you begin? Prayer. Who has time for prayer? Martin Luther was once asked his plans for the day. He replied, "Work, work, from early until late. In fact, I have so much to do that I shall spend the first three hours in prayer" and Martin Luther knew busy times! Personal, uninterrupted prayer time inculcated with planned Bible reading will help transform those personal audiences with the God, omnipotent Creator the universe to times of sweet communication about anything that is on your heart. It will prepare you to meet the challenges and opportunities the Lord lays before you each day. He will prepare your heart just as you have prepared mentally, physically and emotionally. Paul also wrote in Ephesians chapter six about putting on the whole armor of God. It is the armor you need hanging in your locker ready to put on before you ever begin your shift.

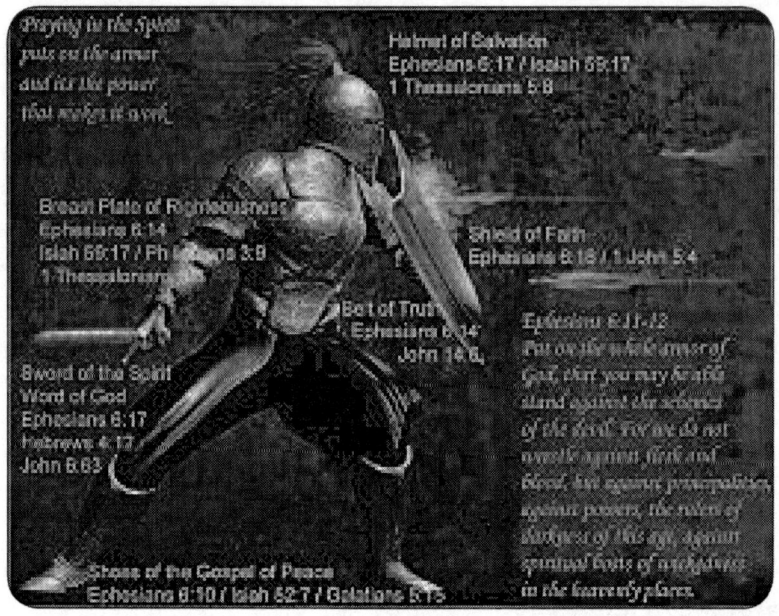

The Bible also informs us iron sharpens iron. The best way for the soldiers of the early centuries to sharpen their weapons was by striking them against iron. The lesson for us is that we must meet with those of similar faith to study the Bible and sharpen ourselves. I have found as a Bible teacher for small groups for many years, as a pastor and now as adjunct faculty for a seminary, I gain as much, or more, than my students as I prepare for the teaching time and we discuss the passages and their author's original meaning.

The author of Hebrews said, "…not forsaking our own assembling together, as is the habit of some, but encouraging one another; and all the more as you see the day drawing near." The *day* he is referring to is the rapture of the church for after that day, there will be no Christian influence at all on earth and no Holy Spirit holding back evil. Such practices are extremely

worthwhile for Christian cops to get together. Have you noticed, if you are one of those who do take part in such times of iron on iron together, that whenever you do, something during that day will relate to what you have studied?

Figure 1 Cops to Haiti in Bible Study with Local Police

There are groups dedicated to working with Christian cops, mostly made up of cops. Groups provide materials for study, outreach on social media and many go on specific mission trips to work with cops in other countries. Most of the time the groups will teach in an academy type of environment and then when it comes to free time, the officers can share their testimonies and talk about the things of faith. Just a short list of those groups are:

Peace Officers for Christ International (POFCI)

www.pofci.com

Christian Police Association – USA (CPA-USA)

www.cpa.com

Fellowship of Christian Police Officers (FCPO)

www.fcpo.com

Peace Officer Ministries (POM)

www.peaceofficerministries.org (provides retreats for law enforcement and study materials)

International Christian Police Fellowship (ICPF)

www.internationalcpf.org

Note: The author only lists these organizations based on their web presentations. It is up to the reader to determine the validity of each in which they have an interest.

RETAKING THE CASTLE

When I have the honor of not just marrying a couple but taking them through several sessions of pre-marriage counseling, one of the topics is titled *Protecting the Castle* which is based on the adage *your home is your castle*. My admonition to them to help them keep their homes safe from on-slaught of the world is to *keep the drawbridge up and the moat full!* Here though, we need to honestly discuss *'Retaking the Castle'*.

Keeping the Drawbridge Up

It is sometimes difficult to tell what will attempt to invade our castle and rob you of the spiritual peace and strength you strive to keep. If you do not maintain your own central vision on God and His work in your life, those with false doctrine, those who seek to stir up trouble and create doubt will attack your castle where God's presence should be forever realized. I first wrote the word *felt* instead of *realized* but feelings are fickle and Satan can twist feelings all around to make you doubt God's promises. Christ promised He would *never leave or forsake you.* If your home is strong, you can be strong. If you are strong, your place in the thin-blue line is strong. If you are helping to stretch that thin blue line then look for the strength in others so as to match strengths when the line is set in battle formation. At a minimum, seek out a civilian who has notable potential and is teachable. Iron sharpens iron.

Keeping invaders out of your castle requires more than a *Mom and Pop Security System.* That is, either you or your spouse's parents (or both) were strong in their Christian faith and their marriage lasted their entire lives so you'll mimic what you saw them do on the outside and make it work on the inside of your castle.

Keeping your castle secure requires more than a single *court clergy.* By this we refer to the idea that there is one person the family who is walking with God. Everyone in the family will depend on him for all spiritual needs without ever seeking a walk of their own. A strong family, all walking with God is what is necessary to keep that castle secure.

Keeping your castle secure requires diligence about who you allow into its walls. The Spirit will help you keep a discerning spirit. This is particularly important in the friends your teens bring home and the guy that comes to date your daughter. What kind of man is he now? Where will he lead your daughter? If you have a son who is dating then the question becomes, "Where will she lead your son?

ACTION STEPS

From time to time in the text as we get into the heart of what needs to be done in order to maintain the principle that is being described.

1. *Pray* - Okay, you say that sounds like a cop-out because I promised early on this would not be a soft-soap kind of text. Well, here's the catch. If your son or daughter is still a small child, perhaps he or she is not even born yet; I want you to begin praying now for them. Begin praying for their salvation now! Pray every day for them, for their lives, their walk with God and watch how He blesses you for it. Also pray for who they will marry. How that young man or lady is raised will make a world of difference in how they will parent their family; therefore if you care about your grand-children you'll remind yourself of these simple steps to help keep your castle secure.

2. *Meet Often with the Knights of the Round Table* This is a measure of accountability. We have said Christians must not give up meeting together; there is much to be said for corporate worship and corporate study. But, the Knights of the Round Table is much more intimate. In Medieval times the knights were people the king could truly trust. As much as they were dedicated to him; they were even more so to

the crown or we might say in this biblical reference, they are your friends but they are dedicated to the Gospel. They are ready to graciously *call you on it* when you begin to step out of bounds. If you're struggling with a sin, you need a group of men or an individual man (women for women) with whom you can be open and they to you. You agree to hold each other accountable for your actions.

We are going to turn this next instructional panel (cartoon) around to look at it from the point of view of the dragons. Either

the castle owner has put the dragons in for protection or his castle has been overrun by the nefarious dragons and he must take his castle back. Since the title of this section is *RETAKING the CAS-TLE,* let's assume the dragons are interlopers and the castle must be retaken by the gallant Hagar. As it is in many of government entities, Hagar is the type of leader who will attempt to promote a false positive in order to keep the morale of the employees' alive. When we strive to retake our castles, we cannot attempt to promote false positives to our families. If we, as fathers or mothers have not held up our end of the responsibilities for leading spiritually in the home; then we need to confess that openly to our family and commit to do better. Let them know you have accountability partners to help you do it and tell the family you will be having Bible times for yourself and for the family. That you will seek out a Bible teaching church and begin not just attending but getting involved. Trust, too, that you need not make a show of your private Bible times with God. He prefers you go off in secret. Your family will notice and appreciate your efforts eventually *in God's timing.*

A QUICK REVIEW

> ➢ *Yourself- get a plan to stay spiritually healthy*
> ➢ *Your family and castle - expand that plan to include all who reside in the castle*
> ➢ *Your work- Make certain you are the same person at work that you are at home– this is more difficult than it sounds.*
>> o *Ask the guys at work to exclude you from certain jokes, stories and the like.*
>> o *You don't need to evangelize with every conversation but use the biblical principle of:* "In the same way, let your light shine before others, that they may see your good deeds and glorify your Father in heaven."

Now that you have committed yourself to the retaking of the castle and getting your own Knights of the Round Table prepared, it is time to move into the new adventure of preparing to stretch the thin blue line to include a new type of centurion. Together, citizens of every town and the citizens who are also cops in that town will form a first line of defense against the heightened threat. It requires communities to understand the depth of the enemy's passion to devastate its adversaries. Once there is a comprehension as to the threat there will be either a mass exodus from the ranks of volunteers or there will be more volunteers than for which you are prepared. Knowing Americans as I believe I do, my wager is on the latter.

In early December of 2014 jihadists claimed to have smuggled a dirty bomb (radioactive device) into a city somewhere in Europe. A former Pentagon advisor, Michael Rubin argued that counterterrorism officials should take note of what is being claimed by the ISIS confidants. "Too often, counterterrorism officials plan to prevent replication of the last terror attack," Rubin said. "Terror groups, however, plan to shock with something new." The concept of an actual dirty bomb being in a highly-populated area is almost unbelievable. When it is combined with other intelligence, the reality sets in. "Iraq reportedly informed the United Nations in July that terrorists had seized nuclear materials being housed at Mosul University. Some 90 pounds of uranium were said to have been stolen, according to reports." The threats are real. Rubin went on to say, "The threats also should factor into the ongoing debates about border control, according to Rubin. "Perhaps it's also time to recognize that open borders and successful counter-terrorism are mutually exclusive," he said. "It's a lesson that might fly in the face of (former President) Obama's ideology, but reality will always trump political spin."

The need for New Centurions is real.

The Citizen Centurions

How do we begin to create the Citizen Centurions? A brief review of some of the plans, programs and pitfalls of the previous attempts to expand the law enforcement capability for jurisdictions is in order. From the very beginning there have been volunteers, police reserves, auxiliary and part time officers but each and every one of these had as their goal the addition of *manpower* to the agency with as little cost as possible. There have been exemplary persons (male and female regardless of the word *manpower*) in each of those roles. However, more often it was the case these individuals were not well trained prior to the introduction of mandatory training standards across states and local jurisdictions. The equipment was sometimes handed down or older equipment left at the department from a generation before, not unlike many of the 1970's military reserve units. The key, though, is the limited vision of the goal of these programs.

In many jurisdictions today, there are what is known as Citizen Police Academies. These can be more than just a public relation move by a local sheriff, prosecutor or chief of police. The amount of contact local business persons who attended an academy have with police agencies after their graduation is little. Schedules and life interfere and the end result is the information passed along is good and may be beneficial in garnering support for the police for financial or political concerns but as far as adding to the length, width or strength of the thin blue line.

The best option before jumping on another *Neighborhood Watch* or *Citizens' Crime Watch* program is to define very specifically what the goal is for bringing Citizen Centurions into your portion of the *thin blue line*. Crime and Neighborhood Watch programs can be very effective as far as they go and may even be an initial source of applicants for the Citizen Centurions. Still, they are just what the term means, *programs*. Their purposes are usually two-fold. The first is to foster communication between police and citizens in areas that had more than their share of crime or crimes of very high visibility where police needed to show some kind of action plan. The second is being a program, something the police can offer its community. It comes with signs and letters, titles and some responsibility, but mostly the *prestige*, if you will, to have been selected for such a program.

One example of the purpose behind a *Citizens' Police Academy* states: "The Citizens Police Academy is a program to reach out to our community to familiarize citizens with the inner workings of the Southaven Police Department and emergency services through lectures and tours of facilities and divisions within our agency and others. This course provides citizens the opportunity to understand how to further contribute to their community and work with the Southaven Police Department more effectively in the prevention of crime."

These are not bad things in and of themselves but for some who become involved they are the *end* they were seeking and little else would come from it. The City of Southaven Mississippi whose example is used here appears to be very pro-active in getting the citizens and the community communicating. There are over 31 different departments or activities that can directly notify by *SMS* any citizen who signs on to receive them including emergency alerts. There is a way to track citizen comments and what is done about requests or concerns and the police department is doing *Safety City* and *Neighborhood Watch* as well as their Citizens' Academy. Anytime the folks who are working for the citizens by being employed by the municipality are actually talking face to face with the individual citizens that is a positive move in the right direction. Southampton should be applauded for their efforts and if they desire to keep moving forward, it would not be surprising they would be very interested in the concepts defined here.

Though all of this may seem very critical of these efforts; the point is not to denigrate the many good things that have resulted from the many hours and dedicated work of police and citizens together. What is critical to understand is the level of the threat currently facing this country is so great no previous *program* was ever designed to confront such peril. The Citizen Centurions will be asked to help local law enforcement agencies grapple with an extremely difficult challenge. It is a task that has become much more familiar now to the U.S. military with their decades in the Middle East working with IEDs and terrorist attacks on a regular basis. The commonalities of the attacks have been delineated and the characteristics of what to look for prior to an attack have been diligently mapped, studied and gathered for education and dissemination to allies in the *war against terrorists.*

DEFINING THE THREAT IN HUMAN TERMS

Take note of the term just used, *war against terrorists.* In WWII, the Nazis used a method of warfare they called the *Blitzkrieg.* The German word means literally *lightning war* and described their ability to attack suddenly, fiercely and relentlessly which allowed them to make large battlefield gains rapidly. The U.S. military never fought a *War on Blitzkrieg,* but, they fought a war against the Nazis and Axis Powers. The U.S. is not fighting a *War on Terror,* but they are fighting a war *against terrorists.* It is more than a matter of semantics. To fight a *War on Terror,* we must picture ourselves going up against a huge, faceless, person-less, horror like the boogey-man in your closet at night when you are a child.

To fight and defeat an enemy, it must be a person or an entity with a face or a cause embodied by persons who fight for it and who have failures and weaknesses and do not have the omnipotence that a horrific *ghost warrior* might have. When we make the enemy this faceless *force*, we assign the terrorist a power he does not have. Unwittingly, he is elevated by us to such a degree as to evoke fear from us. Most of the time, however, he is a misfit from society that seeks either some virgin filled fantasy-world or just wants someone from his pathetic hometown to notice him and to give him some level of importance he never achieved in his daily life. Some may be truly dedicated to their faith and believe their actions will give them a chance at immortality. In rational thought, however, who allows someone else to tell them how glorious it is to strap on a bomb and blow-up an infidel when the person describing the glory to be had has never done it (and is not willing to do it) himself?

There is a balance here that must be maintained. A few paragraphs ago, it was proposed the enemy is feckless and only looking for some pathetic form of recognition. That type of a description is often correct when looking at the individual fighters and it is great for a locker room pep talk at half-time; but, underestimating the enemy can have deadly consequences. Soldiers and citizens alike must not allow the propaganda of either the enemy, himself, or a zealous proponent of the kill 'em all and let God sort it out mentality to weigh one more heavily than the other. An analysis of the enemy's strength based on facts is critical. At the same time, those facts must be filtered through the HUMINT analysis process to determine its validity. It is important to realize, for example, that ISIS or the Islamic State at this point is growing stronger and more determined than ever. The Independent journalist, Jürgen Todenhöfer, who at the age of 74 recently traveled through Syria and Mosul uncovering as much detail about ISIS as possible, was imbedded with ISIS for ten days and is reporting on his findings. He stated the Allies definitely are underestimating

ISIS and they have plans for a mass genocide. Todenhöfer, who is German reported as early as July 2012 that al Qaeda was throughout Syria. He is the first western journalist allowed an inside look at ISIS. Of course, one should expect they would try to use him for propaganda. His reporting portrays ISIS as a strong enemy of the west but he has the background and credentials to allow readers to give ample credence to his report when he tells them there is more here than what the media has uncovered previously. According to the report, "Once within Isis territory, Todenhöfer said his strongest impression was "that Isis is much stronger than we think here". He said it now has "dimensions larger than the UK", and is supported by "an almost ecstatic enthusiasm that I have never encountered in any other warzone. Each day, hundreds of willing fighters arrive from all over the world," he told (German website *Der tz*). "For me it is incomprehensible."

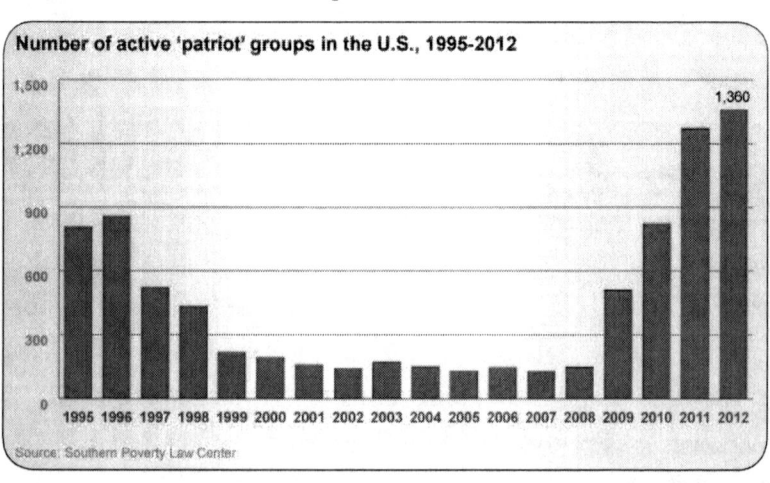

Number of active 'patriot' groups in the U.S., 1995-2012

Source: Southern Poverty Law Center

Once the enemy is a human, whether a zealot for Islam from the Middle East or an anti-government extremist from California, he is fallible and able to be defeated. Along those lines, it is important to note that just as the threat from terrorist cells with ISIS is growing, so too are the number of anti-government hate groups in the U.S. according to research by the Southern Poverty Law Center. The previous chart indicates the numbers of Anti-Government *patriot* hate groups is growing in the United States.

One author warns the readers to not take too much stock in the numbers. "Jesse Walker, of the Reason Foundation and author of an upcoming book, "The United States of Paranoia: A Conspiracy Theory," said counting groups isn't a good way to measure the threat. 'It's dubious to assume growth in numbers is related to violence.'"

It is always a matter of definition for what constitutes a hate group. The Southern Poverty Law Center has been known to be very generous as to what groups they will allow into the cult or hate group category. An admonition of *caveat emptor* is appropriate anytime you read an analysis based on statistics. The following is one such analysis.

CNN announced that: "A report released Tuesday by the Southern Poverty Law Center counted 1,360 "patriot" extremist groups in 2012 -- up by 7% from 2011. The study defines patriot groups as anti-government militias driven by their fear that authorities will strip them of their guns and liberties." As local law enforcement then, based on your own local conditions, your experiential history with groups will often dictate how much credence is given to similar reports. It is necessary to weigh the intelligence and the experiential data to determine their relevance. Once these have been sifted through your grid, the next key issue becomes knowing how to best prepare for the coming threats and to gather additional intelligence from all aspects. This will enable law enforcement authorities to develop the best picture for what may certainly be inflicted upon the local communities in the near future. An additional cause for concern is the impact that years of struggle have had upon veterans of the war against criminals and terrorists.

War Weary

Recently two long time soldiers from the front lines of the war on terrorists and the battles to keep crime and drugs out of our local communities approached me with comments that I have never heard from them in over thirty years of fighting the good fight. The conversations were at separate times and one knew nothing of the other's comments. The faces and the tone of their voices revealed a weariness that betrayed the number of years these veterans have battled. The determination to fight against the evil that preys upon the citizens has taken a serious hit when noble veterans are pushed to the point of despair. The source of such weariness is a two-pronged issue that comes *not* from law enforcement and the criminal justice system being *unable* to wage the war and to carry out a strategy for success. Rather, it comes from the obstacles that seem to be infinitely thrown in the paths of these brave warriors, not by the enemies of our society, but from those who should be our allies.

In a section in the latter half of this work is a discussion of the media's role in this war and how vital a unified approach is to gather and maintain public support for the efforts. That does not mean law enforcement actions that go beyond what is lawful are white-washed by a friendly media but it does mean that the media works to find ways to support law enforcement in its role and does not throw cops under the bus for the sake of a good headline and increased sales.

The second prong of the problem is administrations within local, state and federal governments that do not grasp the enormity of the issues. Politicians sacrifice an effective strategy by turning immediately to law enforcement budgets when looking for places to garner political points by slashing already bare-bones budgets. Thankfully this is not true of *every* politician or *every* government; there are many dedicated to the struggle and they understand the risks involved in not keeping a strategic force capable of facing an unrelenting foe.

It has always been true that whenever a major crime boss or nefarious drug dealer is taken out of the equation, sooner or later another would-be villain steps into his place. It is also true that eventually God will bring an end to the struggles and evil will once and forever be destroyed. Until that time comes, however, it is the valiant soldiers of the front lines that must continue to battle an unrelenting foe and keep away the predators from our communities as best we can. The actual definition of the *thin blue line* is quite appropriate. It is that line between civilization and anarchy. To say it is of no use; gloom and despair have won is tantamount to surrender which nullifies the supreme sacrifice made by so many already in this war. That is unacceptable. One argues we should discourage the best and the brightest among us from enlisting in the battle. Does that mean there are some who are *expendable* and therefore it is they who can go and fight on behalf of those who are *too good to go?* I know that neither of the veterans who spoke with me would argue for such a thing. It was,

I am certain, fatigue and frustration that caused them to vent their feelings in such a way. If the battle was young for them and they were new to the fight, they would still be the first to make their mark and join the forces for good.

In the Charles Dickens classic, *A Christmas Carol,* the Ghost of Christmas Past declares: "'I told you these were shadows of the things that have been,' said the Ghost. 'That they are what they are, do not blame me!'"

The focus of the specters' visits, Ebenezer Scrooge, later is told by the Ghost of Christmas Present that, if the conditions did not change for the Cratchets, by the next Christmas Tiny Tim's seat by the fire would be empty and his crutch would be without an owner. It is true beyond the words of a writer like Charles Dickens that the shadows of the past are what they are. The Apostle Paul writes, in his letter to the church at Philippi, "...forgetting those things which are behind and reaching forward to those things which are ahead, I press toward the goal for the prize..." If we are to continue the battle against the forces of evil and to seek to make our communities safer in the days ahead then they are right at this very moment, we cannot be defeated by the hard fought, yet lost battles of the past. Those days are what they are. We must recall there were many wondrous days and many victories helping to carry the days ahead. The Apostle Paul's goal was the *upward call of God in Christ.* Ours, not as eloquently said, perhaps as Paul's, but the work of law enforcement is still to protect the weak, the children, the infirm and the elderly. Not excluded is the remainder of society that looks to their local police to help to dispel the fear that comes in the night when thoughts of what terrorists and other evil men can do. We must, then, learn from the past; from the victories and the defeats and steel ourselves for the future. The *Blue,* from retired veterans to the newest *New Centurion,* must prepare to do battle and face the threat.

HOW TO FACE THE THREAT AS A LOCAL LAW ENFORCEMENT AGENCY

A search of several criminal justice books revealed no one as having laid claim to being the creator of the analogy of a *thin blue line.* We will continue with the definition presented earlier, the last line of defense between civilization and anarchy, as the groundwork for what we build here.

Police work or law enforcement has undergone a myriad of changes in its lifetime. Without going as far back as Hammurabi and his writing of a code of law or to the Greek city-states where in their language *polis* meant city and those who cared for it to watch over it and protect it from harm were from within that community, so the word *polis* is so appropriate for *police.* It should be noted here that eventually in many of the early civilizations either the captured slaves or indentured servants were the ones who kept the watch. The rich could buy their way out of having to do their *turn* to *watch* but the poor could not so eventually it was often the non-citizen poor. Still, the Greeks had a better idea. Similar to Nehemiah, that was mentioned earlier, they knew those who were protecting something of value to them would do a better job of it. Nehemiah went so far as to assign those who were rebuilding the broken walls of Jerusalem to rebuild the portions in front of or nearest their own homes as that way they would do a better job. When protection was needed, one man would work and another stood with a weapon ready to stop any intruders. And so it was that as time progressed eventually *new and improved methods* of police work were sought.

Early in the 20th Century, two men, August Vollmer and Orlando Wilson, contemporaries of one another, developed the idea that police needed to be more a part of their communities. The *rapid response* that police in vehicles had created also the result of developing a wedge between citizens and police with communication between them. Wilson and Vollmer were making good strides in that protection. Fortunately for those cheering on Wilson and Vollmer in their quest for professionalization of police services and the strengthening of the tie between citizens and their ability to solve cases, they would make some serious in-roads before J. Edgar Hoover would attempt to re-make law enforcement in his own image. Serious about professional policing, Hoover saw a large federal role in nationwide policing. He developed academies and training and brought the Federal bureau of Investigation (FBI) into its own during his long tenure. The facts that "More than nine-tenths of arrests, for example, resulted from citizens' requests for police action. Later studies, such as one in Kansas City, Mo., in the mid-1970s, found that preventive patrols by automobile did not effective." (sic) It was not long until, "Vollmer's idealistic vision of police work, with its strong emphasis on social work, was replaced with Hoover's strategy. Instead of broadening police responsibilities as Vollmer had proposed, the new reformers narrowed them to concentrate on fighting serious street crimes. They also moved to sever the close ties between officers and neighbourhoods (sic). Assignments were changed often; officers no longer patrolled areas in which they lived; and, most important, the police began to patrol in automobiles. To insulate police…"

A series of programs throughout the 1970's and 80's began the process of attempting to recreate the connections with citizens lost through the heyday of government control. However, just as all other things in government life, and life in general for that matter, everything seems to have a cycle and soon the era of local control of law enforcement and community based initiatives came to a screeching halt. The horrific acts of 9/11 saw to that. It seemed the grievous methods of terrorists were so large that only the massive force of American power applied with full strength by the federal government was the only appropriate response. Granted, however, at that time it was believed the evil forces behind terrorism were all overseas. It was also believed there was very little connection between the heinous acts of terror and the daily events that could come under the auspices of local law enforcement. There was comfort in the idea of a huge response by massive amounts of military force. To think terrorists could strike in the small hometowns across America was too frightening to imagine and local law enforcement had no idea what the enemy might look like. There were, of course, clashes against anyone who appeared to be Middle Eastern or Muslim and it was fear exacerbated by ignorance that fueled much of the rage. It has taken time and experience for law enforcement to begin to understand the very nature of the enemy. That experience has also shown there are connections that do occur within the confines of small town America. We began to understand how much time the terrorists that flew the planes into the Twin Towers or into a field in Pennsylvania had spent living among Americans that began to open the eyes of local authorities.

SITUATIONAL AWARENESS

The world is a dangerous place. "Although there is danger in the world, one does not have to become resigned to fate and passively wait for acts of violence to occur. There are some simple steps ordinary people can take to help them avoid danger – or to at least mitigate its impact." By initiating tactics such as situational awareness, local law enforcement can become proactive in the war against terrorists and not simply responders to it.

The primary rule taught to *ordinary citizens* is to *avoid* the danger. When the conversation changes to those who are willing to stand with local law enforcement to strengthen the *thin blue line* these citizens are no longer expected to simply avoid the danger but instead to seek it out, confront it and mitigate it in accordance with their training and abilities to protect the rest of the community. The people who are selected as part of the *new blue* must be prepared to take these uncommon steps *toward* the threat.

There are still tools, though that must be applied to make certain the *New Centurion* gets to the danger and is still capable of confronting it. To be wounded, or in some other way kept from reaching the scene of an incident, is to detract substantially from available response resources. Arriving at an incident so physically drained from the obstacles that had to be overcome to arrive there so spent, means this responder is of little to no value. The loss of one responder in this way is more than a loss of personnel in response to the event. It is a drain on the already stressed response units. Now those units must also care for one of their own who is not able to contribute to the resolution of the problem. One such tool that will help insure responders are fully capable on scene is one of tactical preparation.

Tactical preparation begins with *situational awareness.* A couple of basic examples are best for conveying what this is all about. First, understand this is a mindset and as it is practiced it becomes more than just a tool, it becomes a way of living. Once it is second nature, you find you practice it even when you are not 'on duty' and it begins without even thinking about it. This is a good sign you did not leave your training and awareness in your police locker but you have carried these survival techniques over into your daily life. That is an accomplishment worth celebrating and a characteristic that needs to be honed and practiced daily so you never lose it.

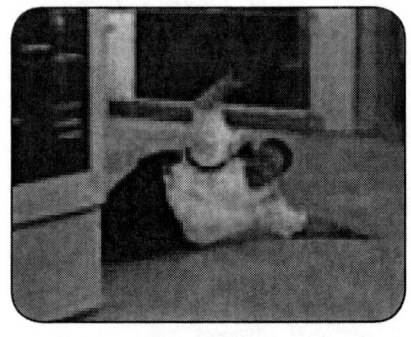

Situational awareness is not a comical lunging from light pole to light pole for cover while walking down Main Street or a *Paul Blart Mall Cop,* sliding across the wax floor to gain cover. *It is* parking your car outside the bank in a place where you can walk past the window and gain a preview of activity inside the bank before you walk in to a hold-up in progress. It is glancing in the shop windows as you walk down Main Street to see who it is behind you and when you do find yourself in the presence of people who send a warning bell to your survival senses, immediately you go into a *protect mode* and you do not forget to continually *be aware of their hands.* Situational awareness is walking into a convenience store and scanning the interior for someone who appears nervous, out of place or continually looking back out the window as if receiving cues or directions from someone outside or waiting for someone else to arrive. It is noticing someone who appears to be wearing a coat in warm weather to either conceal stolen goods or to be hiding a firearm. Situational awareness includes positioning yourself so you can always see the doors and have as few people as possible able to move behind you. Such a tactic is a common method for keeping situational awareness front and center in your everyday life without bordering on paranoia. If you do not believe such techniques are utilized, watch the next time you are with a cop or more than one cop and see how they vie for who will sit with their back to the door. They all prefer to have their back to the wall facing the door and preferably be able to view the cash register at the same time. Often, when cops are together with their regular police partners there will be less competition for the seat because they have learned to trust one another to *watch their backs.* When those cops are out, though, with untrained or unknown persons, the move for the chair by the wall will occur infamously quickly, sometimes barely perceptible to the uninformed.

There are times, though, it may not be that discreet! If you talk with the spouses of law enforcement officers, you will regularly hear they have learned to relinquish the strategic seat to their spouse without a word between them. While they are being seated, the veteran cops will also have already scanned the room for anyone they know who is trouble, looked for and found any couple involved in a low-key disagreement, or other signs of potential trouble. Many would be able to even give you a head-count of the patrons in a place with one sweep of the room. Understanding the importance placed upon situational awareness is aided by comprehending its usefulness.

Think in terms of being able to describe the situation you found yourself in to a group who was nowhere near the situation and has never placed themselves in harm's way, especially for a stranger. How would you convey what it was which made you sense your life or someone else's life was about to be in serious danger? The terms you choose to make that argument are some of the key words for situational awareness. In the courtroom, if an officer has acted, something as simple as stopping someone along a sidewalk in a neighborhood to do a field interview of them; if that citizen brings a complaint to the department or the courts, the judging authorities will expect the officer to provide *an articulable suspicion.*

The officer has to put into words exactly what it was that made the hair on the back of his neck stand-up or what gave him a sense something was just *not right.* If he cannot put that suspicion into words and make it obvious for the average person to understand, the officer will have difficulty vindicating himself from the complaint. Articulable suspicion is far below the probable cause standard needed to make an arrest but it is more than a hunch. It is the totality of the circumstances, the context in which the event is being played out, the person's clothing, the time, the location, the person's demeanor when approached or before and can include knowledge the officer might have about previous events in a given location that make the person being there even more suspect.

If there must be a single skill inculcated in the *New Centurions,* it is this situational awareness. It will keep the new rookie alive, it may keep the cops around him or her alive, it may protect an untold number of citizens and most of all it will likely keep all of the families of those who might otherwise have suffered greatly from having to mourn their loss. Situational awareness has been described as being aware of one's surrounding and identifying potential threats and dangerous situations and that it is more of a mindset than a hard skill. Anyone can be taught the basic actions that, when practiced regularly, become a habit and those habits will become a part of a person's everyday activity.

According to one source, "Situational awareness is not only important for recognizing terrorist threats, but it also serves to identify criminal behavior and other dangerous situations." Bad things happen. That is a fact of life. Your awareness may help you avoid them and it may even help you prevent them. One would-be robber told police he had started to rob a particular establishment but there were a couple of people there who paid a great deal of attention to him and he knew they would be able to identify him, so he moved on to somewhere else where people were less likely to be looking up from their phones or more focused on their own problems in their own world in the zombie like state of most rush hour commuters on a downtown Manhattan subway at 5:30.

Who are you counting on to protect you when bad things happen to you? Denial by saying bad things are not going to happen to you or the chances are so remote it is not worth considering is dangerous and can be deadly. As equally dangerous are denial's cousins, apathy and complacency. Perhaps you are one of those who really, truly does not care if something bad happens to you. Are you as equally apathetic about bad things happening to those you love, such as your children or grandchildren? No? Then who are you expecting to protect them when you are with them if it cannot be you? Perhaps you are a fatalist. That is part of being complacent. It is a '*Tout ce qu'il sera sera*' attitude. Again, to say for yourself, *what will be will be,* is one thing; but, are you willing to accept it for your loved ones, particularly the children who are so defenseless?

In one method of self-defense presented many years ago, the trainer implores the person being attacked to get very angry at the attacker for the hurt they are about to cause your family if they hurt you. The premise was the anger will increase your ability to respond exponentially. How accurate that such a mindset is truly effective is open for debate; but, there is no doubt that just as a mother bear will go off the charts in protecting her cubs, emotions will impact your ability to react and to survive. Having an excellent capability for situational awareness will help keep you out of circumstances that require you to choose how best to defend against a surprise attacker.

The concept of who you are going to expect to protect you if you do not protect yourself was mentioned in the first part of this section. Just exactly upon who are you relying? If someone is of the mindset to be part of the *New Blue* and the strengthening of the *Thin Blue Line* then already they are of a mindset to be protecting themselves, their family and their community. Sadly, however, many individuals out there decry the police, disdain the military but yet have no idea what they would ever do if they should find themselves in harm's way. Suddenly, the cops who are too militaristic and the military who are too much of a goose-stepping fascist sort look pretty good to them if they just happen down the road at that moment. Everyone in America, it seems, is expecting to go to bed safely at night, sleep undisturbed during the night, and the next morning awake to find all their precious property in pristine shape just as they left it the night before. Yet, those cops who work the night shift are disliked, untrusted and defamed whenever possible it seems by some faction of today's society that has enough pull to make headlines much of the time. Perhaps that is some hyperbole but, not much. Once a person becomes situationally aware, they also realize (usually) there is only one person in the entire world they can count on for their protection twenty-four hours a day, seven days a week and three hundred and sixty-five days a year. That person is themselves. That person is also most likely to be a good candidate for the *New Centurions* and is ready to begin some real training.

Situational Awareness is perhaps the primary characteristic that is needed to be able to train someone for the methodology we are calling for lack of a better name, *New Centurions*. Training and experience are excellent resources, in fact they are irreplaceable. However, the Situational Awareness (SA) mindset is an intangible quality. Some of the characteristics of *what SA is* can be taught. However, to incorporate it into someone's own tool belt so well that it becomes nearly a subconscious behavior is more of a gift than a skill. It comes as a box set with another characteristic and that is what has been called by some *a cop sense* or *spider senses, gut feelings* or more broadly *intuition*. An example from many years ago may help explain what is meant by *cop sense*.

After my initial training with the U.S. Air Force Reserve, I began working as a security officer for a small mid-western college. We were a patrolling security force and we handled basic calls such as theft complaints, misdemeanor infractions and initial response even to felonies. We also performed some basic security services. One midnight shift, I drove past a specific building not on our 'regular check' sheet – that was it did not require a walk-around check unless there had been some previously planned event there and we then we would *lock up* when it was done. This particular night there was nothing planned there and certainly no reason to walk the building. I could not shake this sudden unsettledness I felt as I drove by. It was like an invisible force was drawing me there and in my mind, I just knew something was not right. I radioed to dispatch that I would be on foot checking the building. As I rounded the back corner of the building I saw where a break-in had just occurred, there was broken glass, an open window and one set of muddy footprints on the window ledge. I notified dispatch of the situation and waited for local police back-up. One veteran lieutenant came up to me after the event was over and simply said, '*Well, you're beginning to get 'em.*' I asked him what he meant and he replied, '*Cop Senses.*' He was right and throughout the next few decades working patrol, those senses helped me more than I can begin to relate here. A very large part of that sense is situational awareness.

Scott Stewart writing for **Stratfor-Global Intelligence**, wrote situational awareness is "More mindset than skill." His point was that "It is important to note the situational awareness – being aware of one's surrounding and identifying potential threats and dangerous situations – is more of a mindset than a hard skill. Because of this, situational awareness is not something that can be practiced only by highly trained government agents or specialized corporate security teams."

It takes the will to practice it and the discipline to continue to work at it. This is particularly true when day after day and even month after month there are no results of which to speak. Still, one must remain willing to continue to watch and wait. Such a skill will be extremely useful for those involved in law enforcement in identifying criminal behavior and as a safety tool to identify danger before it is too late.

There is a scene in the John Wayne film, El Dorado when the Duke is waiting for his supper in a small cantina near the Texas and Mexico border. Across from him at a table is another professional *gunslinger* who has three of his men with him. Duke is keenly aware of them and in walks another man who is definitely out of place. He has on an odd hat for that area of the country and he has no sidearm. As this man walks around the table with the gunslinger and his three men, the second gunslinger's eyes never leave the man and the Duke quietly instructs the Cantina girls sitting at his table to vamoose. The three 'un-professional' gang members at the table are preoccupied and never even notice the man until he calls one of them out by name. By the time he challenges the one hired hand and kills him by throwing a hidden knife from behind his head, already the Duke has his gun ready and is prepared to act if necessary. *Situational awareness* comes with experience and will be a skill that confirms the precept the best way to survive a dangerous incident is to **Avoid It.** The Duke gives the young man two pieces of advice, since he admits he struggles with staying out of trouble. The first was to "get rid of that hat" and "learn to use a gun." The *Mississippi gambler's hat* the young man wore was an example of improperly drawing attention to oneself. Bringing only a knife to a gunfight is a sure way to lose most of the time. The Duke's advice though about that hat brings up the tactic of being *gray*.

THE GRAY MAN

The extension of situational awareness into methodologies for personal protection can be found in the concept of *the gray man*. In the 1970's the terror of choice was the airplane hijacking. The number of hijacked airliners and the death count growing steadily lead to a great number of studies and conclusions. There were good studies and poor ones; good conclusions and inane ones. One particular concept had the potential to be the beginning of a great thought. That is the art of being the *gray man*. One of its key selling points was that it was going to be applicable across several different types of threats. The concept of becoming gray has to do with visibility. As I have become, as they say, *long in the tooth*, I have become gray but not the way in which it is meant here. Becoming gray is the ability to be unseen even in the wide open, in areas like an airport terminal or in a shopping mall. To be unseen without needing camouflage or artificial concealment is the art of being *the gray man*.

Some of the most obvious failures at this were the overseas travelers in the 1970's when much of the world had gotten their backs up at Americans in general. Much has been said about the *ugly American tourists* and it really did not have to do with looks but with attitudes. During these days of more international travel by regular Americans, there were among the travelers those patriots who covered their luggage in the red white and blue. As many indicators of the feckless American as possible adorning every piece of luggage or clothing. Others wore their faith on their sleeve, or any place else they could pin the biggest most spectacular forms of *Christian jewelry* as they headed into cultures that were anything *but* Christian. The unsuspecting traveler made themselves, and their luggage, targets for every small-time thief and to more sophisticated criminals working in extortion and kidnapping. They were unprepared for a world in which they were the prey and that simple discussions with strangers in open places would lead to hotel rooms burgled. The response was to teach those who were regular travelers how to fly beneath the radar. To successfully travel without making oneself the target of criminals both professional and the petty thieves the Americans needed to become gray. It was part dressing down while toning down one's conversations and, in part, allowing someone else to be the more tempting target. Some studies went so far as to recommend the best seats to take on an airplane to be less likely singled out by hijackers for abuse. If you can imagine what some of the worst places to have to sit on the plane are then you will find the seats most recommended for remaining out of the hijacker's line of site. It became a choice. Sit in the most inconvenient seat on the plane in case it gets hijacked or take your chances and choose that aisle seat two rows back from the exit anyway.

Somewhat surprisingly, the U.S. Department of State has come up with a fairly good list of considerations for surviving a hijacking which can apply to other types of terrorists' attacks. The law enforcement officer or a *New Centurion* may not be able to take advantage of all of these if they are, in fact, moving toward an event to end the situation by neutralizing the offender. However, if *off-duty* and with family, some of these safeguards are exactly what need to be followed. We will post them here for your edification and application. SCI's comments are added to some in parenthesis.

- Be aware of what you discuss with strangers or what may be overheard by others. (This is true for law enforcement all of the time. Take a ride in an elevator in a court building and you will learn more by unguarded conversations than by attempting to steal case files!)

- Try to minimize the time spent in the public area of an airport, which is a less protected area. (Any large public area is included with today's world of IED's and homicide bombers)

- Move quickly from the check-in counter to the secured areas. On arrival, leave the airport as soon as possible.

- As much as possible, avoid luggage tags, dress and behavior which may identify you as an American. (Notice some of the luggage and clothing of other travelers and this will make even more sense to you.)

- Avoid obvious terrorist targets such as places where Americans and Westerners are known to congregate. *Remain friendly but be cautious about discussing personal matters, your itinerary or program.

- Leave no personal or business papers in your hotel room. (There are several methods of protecting you and your information in your hotel room. Always leave the TV on when leaving and hang the Do Not Disturb sign so bad guys won't be sure if you are in or out. Avoid rooms on the first floor and above the seventh. One for burglars the other for fire escape. Avoid rooms at the end of hall by stairway. If you are in a difficult country and your room has been pre-assigned when you arrive, ask for a change of rooms – create a reason. This avoids listening devices or interrupts pre-planned attacks.)

- Watch for people following you or "loiterers" observing your comings and goings. (Use your counter-surveillance techniques.)

- Keep a mental note of safe havens, such as police stations, hotels, hospitals. (Always be aware of your location. Don't *wander* when you leave your hotel but go wherever you are going purposely with directions in mind.)

- Avoid predictable times and routes of travel and report any suspicious activity to local police, and the nearest U.S. embassy or consulate.

- Select your own taxi cabs at random. Don't take a vehicle that is not clearly identified as a taxi.

- Compare the face of the driver with the one posted on his or her license.

- If possible, travel with others (whom you know).

- Be sure of the identity of visitors before opening the door of your hotel room. Don't meet strangers at unknown or remote locations.

- Refuse unexpected packages.

(*Carry with you a 'door wedge' alarm for night time safety.)

SURVIVING A HIJACKING – HOSTAGE TAKING – TERRORIST ATTACK

Cliff Montgomery of *SecretsofSurvival.com* who put together the State Department list above also has some great advice on surviving being taken hostage. Here is some of what he had to say:

Normally, the most dangerous phases of a hijacking or hostage situation are the beginning and, if there is a rescue attempt, [at] the end. [Particularly] at the outset, the terrorists typically are tense, high-strung and may behave irrationally. It is extremely important that you remain calm and alert and manage your own behavior.

Try to avoid resistance and sudden or threatening movements [unless it is absolutely necessary]. Do not struggle or try to escape unless you are certain of being successful [or you truly have no other choice].

Consciously put yourself in a mode of . . . cooperation. Talk normally. Do not complain, avoid belligerency, and comply with all orders and instructions.

If questioned, keep your answers short. Don't volunteer information or make unnecessary overtures.

Maintain your sense of personal dignity and gradually increase your requests for personal comforts. Make these requests in a reasonable, low-key manner.

If you are involved in a lengthier, drawn-out situation, try to establish a rapport with your captors, (even criminals find it harder to kill someone they have come to know as a human being not just a chess pawn) avoiding political discussions or other confrontational subjects.

Establish a daily program of mental and physical activity. Don't be afraid to ask for anything you need or want - medicines, books, pencils, paper.

DETECTING

Watching for Watchers

Returning to your role as local law enforcement or as a member of the *New Centurions* from the discussion of surviving a hostage taking, there is a technique which can be employed by local LEOs to detect nefarious activity in its infancy. That activity could certainly be a terrorist incident or it could be other criminal acts such as the hostage taking by extortionists that was just described. In most every endeavor the key to understanding how events unfolded (in the case of reconstructing a crime after the fact) or calculating when and where a crime may occur is to find the common denominator(s) of each and track those. There is one common denominator across almost every crime that includes pre-planning. That common denominator is *Intelligence.* Primarily, at this point in the discussion, the intelligence that will be most commonly used across agencies with varying types of resources to be protected is HUMINT or *Human Intelligence.* HUMINT is a very broad category. Initially, we will be concerned primarily with *surveillance.* Criminals, terrorists, and would-be criminals all must scope out where they intend to commit the act in order to plan for the most opportune time and methods. There will always be, at some point in the pre-planning process, *watchers.* Should anything interrupt the watchers, including a zealous law enforcement officer checking his beat, the criminals will be required to alter their plan. They may alter the timing or, unfortunately for the LEO's they may change the location. I use the word *unfortunately* because had the LEO's been able to watch the watchers without alerting them, they could have stopped the crime or terrorist attack in its infancy. If they are alerted and they change location, LEO's may never know there is a planned attack until the first shock wave of the explosion is felt. Surveillance is one type of Intel. Others will be very effective with certain types of resources and the right people (Centurions) sifting through the information to gain the clues they need.

The Federal Bureau of Investigation describes the tool of intelligence. "(It) is more important than ever in today's threat environment. The threats facing the United States are evolving. Threats are global, and often emanate from transnational enterprises that rely on sophisticated information technology. They transcend geographic boundaries, as well as the boundaries of authorities in the U.S. national security infrastructure. In this threat environment, having the right information at the right time is essential to protecting national security." As such there are specific types of intelligence necessary for those who would seek to interdict terrorists and other criminals whose penchant is to wreak havoc upon society. The methodologies of intelligence gathering are varied. A brief outline of the types of intelligence to be gathered is appropriate here if one is to comprehend the complexities involved in putting the pieces of the puzzle together and identifying the plans of those most devious people.

DETECTION
INTELLIGENCE DISCIPLINES*

There are five main ways of collecting intelligence that are often collectively referred to as "intelligence collection disciplines" or the "INTs."

Human Intelligence (HUMINT) is the collection of information from human sources. (Author's note: A primary method of gaining HUMINT is through *SURVEILLANCE*.)

Signals Intelligence (SIGINT) refers to electronic transmissions that can be collected by ships, planes, ground sites, or satellites. Communications Intelligence (COMINT) is a type of SIGINT and refers to the interception of communications between two parties. U.S. SIGINT satellites are designed and built by the National Reconnaissance Office, although conducting U.S. signals intelligence activities is primarily the responsibility of the National Security Agency (NSA).

Imagery Intelligence (IMINT) is sometimes also referred to as photo intelligence (PHOTINT). The National Reconnaissance

Office designs, builds, and operates imagery satellites, while the National Geospatial-Intelligence Agency is largely responsible for processing and using the imagery.

Measurement and Signatures Intelligence (MASINT) is a relatively little-known collection discipline that concerns weapons capabilities and industrial activities. MASINT includes the advanced processing and use of data gathered from overhead and airborne IMINT and SIGINT collection systems.

The Defense Intelligence Agency's Central MASINT Office (CMO), is the principal user of MASINT data. Measurement and Signatures Intelligence has become increasingly important due to growing concern about the existence and spread of weapons of mass destruction. MASINT can be used, for example, to help identify chemical weapons or pinpoint the specific features of unknown weapons systems. The FBI's extensive forensic work is a type of MASINT. *The FBI Laboratory's Chem-Bio Sciences Unit, for example, provides analysis to detect traces of chemical, biological, or nuclear materials to support the prevention, investigation, and prosecution of terrorist activities. (Emphasis added)*

Open-Source Intelligence (OSINT) refers to a broad array of information and sources that are generally available, including information obtained from the media (newspapers, radio, television, etc.), professional and academic records (papers, conferences, professional associations, etc.), and public data (government reports, demographics, hearings, speeches, etc.).

*Author's note: Portions of this text have been redacted for the sake of clarity and space. Interested readers should view the footnote citation for complete data. No meaning was changed by the redaction.

The key point of any type of intelligence gathered is its accuracy. As part of its accuracy is its timeliness, ability to be individually verified and that it be tactically sound. The *watchers* must be very aware of this need for detailed accuracy.

Developing skill sets to be able to *watch for watchers* is an excellent role for those whose destiny is to become one who stretches the blue line. In the section on **Re-drawing the Thin Blue Line** the selection of New Centurions by skill sets so as to stretch the line systematically and with an over-arching plan in mind rather than just taking volunteers will be addressed. However, determining who among your new teammates will be best suited for the role of watcher watching is critical. This role requires persons of patience and keen observation skills to notice the most infinitesimal of details and changes in watcher activity. This is not a role for the *hard charging – arrest them all and let the judge decide* kind of person. You will want to choose persons who are very detail oriented.

Each role you determine you need for the stretching of your line should have the forethought put into it as to the characteristics of personality, educational skill set and technical skills necessary for the role. Those will also be determined in part by the *A, B, C's* that are your priority targets to be protected which is also covered in an upcoming section. The two factors, the type of priority to be covered and the roles needed to cover those priorities must dictate the person that will be selected for that position. To not do so is to simply replicate the programs of the past that were sufficient for promoting a general public relations program for a department but not for the serious tasks to which these *New Centurions* will be deployed. To quote Shakespeare, who was also quoted by Sherlock Holmes, "The game's afoot: Follow your spirit, and upon this charge Cry 'God for Harry, England, and Saint George!'"

There is, within every planned act whether it is criminal or a logistical military move, the necessity to have eyes on the target. Appropriate preplanning cannot begin until an assessment has been made as to the location, size, stability, security, sentries, access points and vulnerabilities of the target. As critical as this pre-mission information gathering and reconnaissance is it is also one of the first areas of weakness that can be exploited to learn the enemy's intentions and time table. It is this point wherein the *Watchers* gain their first strike advantage. Scott Stewart of the Strategic Forecasting Group makes the point that in some cases, such as letter bombs, pre-mission surveillance is not necessary. He writes, "Some have argued that physical surveillance has been rendered obsolete by the Internet, but from an operational standpoint, there simply is no substitute for having eyes on the potential target – even more so if the target is mobile."

It is true Google Earth makes some of the initial work easier than before with Internet satellite technology. Specifics like access control points and the interior layout of the building is not normally available by Internet.

Depending on the complexity of the planned attack, pre-attack surveillance could be from a few minutes to several weeks. **The key strategic point is simply that while the enemy is surveilling the target, they are vulnerable to being spotted.** This is the point of which the *Watchers* must take full advantage. It also brings up a central point in selection of the *Watchers* and that is the capability of learning every aspect of the possible targets. The better the *Watcher* knows the possible targets the more likely he or she is to recognize when something is amiss or when someone is around who should not be there. They will know the vantage points suitable for watching for intruders. The key will be knowing which targets to assign *Watchers,* the selection of the *Watchers* and the timing of the possible attacks.

THE GAME IS AFOOT

It takes just a few moments of scanning local news or more pointedly the blogs and reports of intelligence operatives and organizations from around the world to realize the rapidly progressing nature of the volatile terrorist acts, reprisals and vicious acts of criminals. A recent such report indicates a "high degree of confidence" that two known terrorist organizations, *The Electronic Intifada* and *Students for Justice in Palestine* "are engaged in terrorist financing from within the United States of America." The report goes on to stipulate that "...with a high degree of confidence that the top-level officials of these organizations are receiving instruction and training from terrorist organizations specifically linked to *Hamas, Hezbollah,* and the *Muslim Brotherhood."* This, of course, is just one small tip of a very large iceberg.

Writing for the Bureau of Justice Assistance, Dr. David Lambert pens the following caution. "Given the ongoing threat to the United States from the Islamic State of Iraq and Syria and the Khorasan Group, coupled with terrorist activities on our own soil, it is clear that the United States needs to take advantage of every counterterrorism strategy we have." As much as I concur with this statement and the premise behind Dr. Lambert's article, I would push even further and stipulate that it is not enough to utilize *every counterterrorism strategy we have* but it is imperative that we take the slogan of the Lay's potato chip company that says, *we'll make more!* The developing of a national brigade of *new centurions* is just that, the making of new counterterrorism strategies.

Dr. Lambert writes, "When it comes to terrorism at home, it is state and local public safety resources that will protect us." He understands local police detect radicalized individuals and groups within their communities and he sees their role as communicating that to homeland security and counterterrorism agencies that are nationwide. I do not necessarily disagree but I do see a much wider role. It is vital specialized personnel are trained at collecting, evaluating, analyzing and disseminating information on suspect activity but too often there has been a bottleneck of information flowing only one direction in the system and that is from the local agencies up and very seldom has there been in the past much information coming back down. When it did it was usually in the form of some feather preening or horn blowing about what the federal agencies or some other task force had been able to stop. Little credit went to those who brought together the information that completed the picture in the puzzle. It is not for credit, of course, the local LEO's do the work they do but a system cannot function effectively with those parameters. If it is possible to bring together a large information *sharing* system and not just a one-way vacuum tube that would be extremely helpful for local agencies tasked to protect their priority infrastructure. There must also be further understanding of the need for individual citizens to be directly involved in their own defense as well as their role in *saying something* when they, in fact, *see something*.

In just the first few weeks of 2015 there have been terrorist fueled incidents across the globe. In a counterterrorism operation in Verviers Belgium three people were killed as police raided a jihadist cell. A top commander of AQAP, Nasr al-Ansi, took responsibility for the vengeance attacks on Charlie Hebdo magazine in Paris. Also in Paris, a 27-year-old municipal police officer was gunned down while investigating a traffic accident. She was shot in the head and the gunman was wearing a bulletproof vest carrying an assault rifle and a handgun. The officer had been on the force for only fifteen days and was unarmed. Another police officer, guarding the Charlie Hebdo offices was also gunned down.

In the U.S. during these same three weeks, a heart surgeon was gunned down by a lone assailant in the hallway of Boston's Brigham and Women's Hospital. In the rural town of Colerain, Ohio near the West Virginia border and in neighboring Green Township, a 20-year-old man was arrested by the FBI after purchasing two Armalite M-15 5.56mm semiautomatic rifles and 600 rounds of ammunition for $1,900 in cash. He was charged with attempting to kill a U.S. government official and possession of a firearm in furtherance of attempted crime of violence. His plan was to launch an attack against the U.S. Capitol in Washington D.C. The FBI also arrested in an unrelated case, two Pakistani brothers who are naturalized U.S. citizens in Fort Lauderdale Florida. They reside in the smaller town of Oakland Park, Florida and have been indicted on charges of conspiring to provide material support and resources to terrorists and conspiring to use a weapon of mass destruction. On January 15th of 2015 they were additionally charged with conspiring to give aid to al Qaeda and AQAP, forcibly assaulting a federal employee and the attempted murder of a federal employee. In New York City in the same month a U.S. citizen, age 33 Wesam El-Hanafi was indicted for providing material support to al Qaeda by traveling to Yemen. An accomplice 34-year-old Sabirhan Hasanoff, age 34 who is a citizen of both the U.S. and Australia was indicted for providing material assistance by performing assignments for al Qaeda while in New York. Hasanoff was a CPA and is alleged to have used his skills to assist al Qaeda. Another case involved individuals traveling to Pakistan to fight against U.S. soldiers in Afghanistan.

In just the same time frame, French officials have released to the media information that sleeper cells in France have been activated by al Qaeda and AQAP. It is reported that these *sleepers* have trained with al Qaeda in Yemen and have focused targets involving primarily local law enforcement officers. If there were any questions about whether viable strategies are needed for local law enforcement to be proactive during this time in America's history, just this small slice of the information should answer all those questions.

Recently, a well-known political and life-style commentator, Ben Stein wrote an article titled "A Free Society Needs Policing". In it, he made several astute observations which speak to the current situation here in America. He writes, "The police are in a nonstop war in which decent society is under attack by thugs and killers." Stein has the international audience and the professional acumen to give him the clout to be able to say pretty much anything he desires. He proves that with this article. In his closing argument, he writes:

"It doesn't really turn out to be complicated. We cannot have a free society without police. With a very few exceptions – very, very few, the police behave with incredible restraint. The vast majority of deaths of blacks in this country are caused by other blacks – not the police… You can think of it in a simple way: What would happen to New Yorkers if Al Sharpton and Bill de Blasio moved to Cuba for good? What would happen if there were no police?"

The central thrust of Mr. Stein's conclusion can be carried, without hyperbole, to our own. That is, within the current generation of college age students, a stable society will require more than a police presence, they will require that police are not seen as on the opposing side of their lives; but as allies in the fight to keep America free. Without that viewpoint, there may not be a generation understanding of the connection between freedom and rights. Those who express a strong desire to have and exercise *their rights* must learn such expression cannot be made without freedom. Only in a free society can an individual express their rights. A free society does not exist within a vacuum. It can only exist in a contextual environment for which brave men and women have suffered, bled, and died to maintain that free state. A society whose young generation does not comprehend that relational tension is likely to see those who uphold the laws which maintain the civil society as enemies of their freedom rather than guardians of it. There must be a method of educating that generation and those who follow as to this relational tension and what it takes to maintain it. Such an education can lead to recruiting quality college age police applicants or, perhaps, *New Centurions* to wage the war that has been placed upon our doorstep. Those who desire to bring that war to us have in their sites some of the most critical infrastructure and high priority locations within our country. One of the first pro-active measures to be taken is to identify those targets. The premise is simple but the implementation is quite complex. Know what it is your enemy wants and where it is located. Then secure those targets as your first preemptive strike against the enemy.

IDENTIFYING YOUR PRIORITY A, B AND C RESOURCES

There are times in which, as a lead planner for your local law enforcement agency, that you must play the role of Alex Mundy. Alex was played in the 1968 television series by Robert Wagner. As a convicted thief, Mundy was used by officials to ferret out those who were after some prized possession. Alex could think like those thieves and know, ahead of time, where they would strike to steal the valuables. It was a common tool in our patrol work that we would try to think ahead of the thieves to know what parts of our business community were most vulnerable. Such thinking is crucial to crime prevention. All one needs to do is look at the homes in your neighborhood as if you were a prowler and you will notice which use good night lighting and which do not; those who keep their bushes trimmed away from their first-floor windows and entry ways and those who do not. It is that mindset you are encouraged to take at this point to begin to think like a terrorist or other criminal whose plan is to destroy human life or disrupt municipal services. To think like them, you must, as was noted early on, *know your enemy*. The primary role of a terrorist is to strike fear, terror into the hearts of his enemy.

 They want their prey to feel so unsafe they cannot continue in their normal daily lives. Panic across the community and an inability to function normally is the true goal of the terrorist.

If you know the mind of your enemy you can know how it is he must want you to be most hurt. You can see through his eyes what it is he wants to take from the community or how he wants to strike fear into your daily lives. When you can see as he sees, you can identify those parts of your local community that are *your* priority A, B, and C resources. Some communities will share similar priorities but priority resources can also be quite divergent. There is no *one size fit all* type of anti-terrorism watch plan. Each community must realize what it is that makes their community unique to the western world. The terrorist will often strike at that uniqueness. Before you assign your A, B and C designations, take the time to see your community through the eyes and with the mind of a terrorist. The use of the A, B, and C designators will be described in more detail once the community review is complete. On one hand, it could be a large western religious institution that will be the target and on the other a *decadent* nightclub that smacks of everything evil a would-be martyr would desire to destroy. It could be at some pop culture nightclub similar to the Dolphinarium in Tel Aviv, February 26, 2005. The Israeli police knew the bomber was enroute there but they became snarled in traffic. The bomb was intended to go off inside by the dance floor, but knowing his pursuers were close, the homicide bomber ran into the crowd of mostly teenagers awaiting entrance into the club; held the book bag bomb over his head and detonated it, killing four and wounding some fifty others. The bomber was Palestinian just like the photo above. He was someone else's child, he may have had a mother who grieved his death. The choices he made touched many lives. The goal of the group who planned the Dolphinarium bombing was simply to derail the Israel-Palestinian peace process that had temporarily halted nearly 4.5 years of violence. No one wins in an act of violence such as this.

To begin considering your town as a terrorist, or as a villain of some other nomenclature,   step outside of your community and look back upon it. One great source is the travel advertisements and the realty market promotions for your town. What you see when you look at these may be exactly what the terrorist, who has never been to your city, sees for the first time. As you look at all the on-line promotions for your city, think about which of the many attributes would the terrorist's mind focus upon to bring fear and panic to the hearts of the citizens or wreak havoc on both the local and regional economy?

Are your city's webpages replete with page upon page of photos of parks, families and children enjoying sports? Do the promoters of your community advocate for the massive steel mill that employs sixty percent of your workforce? How about your local sports team, whether it is school based, amateur or professional? Is it a key source of pride? How about the transportation system? Do the travel sites promote the ease at which commuters travel cross-town? Are there web stories about the amount of people that travel on local subways at given times of day? All of these questions can be posed by just a few moments of studying what others, realtors, webpage designers and travel sites have promoted for your community. As was mentioned, the terrorist may get his first impression of your community through such sites and that is why the best review of what they might target to get at your community will be to seek out what people are seeing about your town on-line.

One obvious example is the town adjacent to the community where my family and I live now. It is Canton, Ohio and it is known internationally for it being the site of the Pro-Football Hall of Fame. Once a year the world comes to Canton, Ohio for the enshrinement of the newest class of enshrines, both players and coaches. If a terrorist wanted an immediate international audience, there would be a window of opportunity for a few days each August where the detonation of a bomb or an active shooter incident would create severe mass casualties and get worldwide attention. If I am a Canton LEO or an event planner's security consultant for the Hall of Fame then certainly my concentration is going to be upon all of the planning and preparation that is going into the current year's celebration. By reviewing the event plans from previous years, too; one can ascertain where vulnerabilities are most notable. Examples of how terrorists have struck in the past should be always at the forefront of the planning. The Hall of Fame parade that is broadcast at least nationally, if not internationally, does not cordon off the parade route from by-standers. Anyone with a few seconds to a minute before police react could toss an IED into the passing cars of the enshrinees. Will such an act change the world's political stage? No. Will it fill hearts and minds of all who see it on live television and repeated ad nauseum for days with hurt, fear and perhaps even a dreadful panic about public events? Quite possibly. It is not possible to cover every contingency but those by which terrorists have struck in the past or the most vulnerable with ease of access should be considered.

Another issue specific to your local community is your local employers. Do they have an international reach with their product? There are a great many corporations that enjoy a world class reputation. What are they saying to the world? Is what they present about themselves bringing them *and your community* the wrong kind of attention, *at least as far as a terrorist is concerned*? The key is to step completely into the shoes of the terrorist. Having taken his point of view, whether it's the political activist or the religious zealot whom the LEO forecaster is attempting to interdict, the LEOs are attempting to identify their most logical targets based on the context of the community. Once this process has been thought through, the resources of the community, including even its children and schools, are then ready to be classified.

University Study

As the classification process begins in earnest, it is important to look at the local universities linked to your community either by locale, student population, or by a substantial alumni population. One example will make the point as it is not necessary to recall the specifics of an example such as this as much as it is the common denominators that such examples contain. Ten or even five years prior to the completion of this work, the principle terrorist examples would have been al Qaeda and its operation from Pakistan under bin Laden and his successors. Since then a variety of off-shoots of al Qaeda have come to the fore and even now what is called at some points ISIS and others simply the *Islamic State* have over-shadowed al Qaeda as a principle threat to a free world. In the near future, the names and players will have changed again; but their tactics, their mantra and their evil will be no less consistent. What is poignant about the following example is the way in which university campuses have been, for centuries, the seedbed of revolutionary thought; for good and much more for evil.

The following monograph was published by me during the time this book was being created. The analogy lies in whether the law enforcement forecaster or terrorist attack prognosticator can see that within their own local communities, safely tucked away on the college campus, future advocates of violence against their own communities may be being cultivated. Freedom of thought and expression is widely appreciated in the United States and college campuses are supposed to be bastions of protection for such expression, though in reality that is usually only true for more left-wing views than conservative ones. Regardless, I am not advocating the squelching of such dialogue; but it is an unwise person who does not remain apprised of what is being taught formally and informally upon their local campuses.

It is from within such halls of higher learning, among the ivy-covered walls are also some of those who may be the best additions to the thin blue line. Even some of the most ardent socialists who may be teaching at that same local university may prove themselves to be also very much aware of the danger that certain actors upon the human stage may cause when fueled with the ravings of some psychopathic tyrant that have caught the imagination of this particular young mind. These professors may become a reluctant yet valuable source for information about what is transpiring upon campus. The other university connection may not carry an alphabet soup of initials after his or her name; but, they may very well have more insight to the goings on within the student body than anyone else on campus. I am referring to those who work in custodial or maintenance services. While I was working, many years ago, as a Security Officer for the College of Wooster in Wayne County Ohio, I depended heavily on those working closely with the students. The custodial staff, as was mentioned, food service personnel, those who work in the mail room or in the student center all have amazing opportunities to learn a great deal about the seething dark underworld of student life. Okay, probably *seething dark underworld* is a bit of hyperbole, particularly for a mid-western private college in the 1970's. The point remains, those who are closest to where the students are living are most likely to know when and where there may be problems. It is important to note that this is true whether the problem is coming from a student or a member of the faculty. If a teacher has gone around the bend on a particular topic such as the Middle East or another cultural hot topic, the students will know it, they will talk about it and they will share it most usually with those they see every day – their housekeeping staff or residence assistants. This is where you find the stretch for your thin blue line. They may help you to uncover activities within the campus life cycle which can become quite distorted by those who seek to bend the minds of young people and put their models and methodologies to the nefarious. The following is an example of a university project gone beyond the norm.

STUDENTS for JUSTICE in PALESTINE – A Not So Silent Threat

If it walks like a… then it's most likely a… According to the intelligence operatives at *Tactical Rabbit*, "the leaders of EI (Electric Intifada) and SJP (Students for Justice in Palestine) have a polished exterior but a hidden agenda that is anti-government, anti-law enforcement, and pro-violence. It is very possible that Hatem Bazian and Ali Abunimah are more than likely to be foreign agents conducting intelligence operations inside the United States." One of the key roles for these highly-polished university based groups is the raising of funds for additional growth and expansion of the SJP's organization increasing its ability to influence impressionable minds of young people experiencing campus life and its diversity for the first time. Young persons can be overwhelmed by the amount of information coming at them from multiple sources, most of whom the students have been taught to respect as persons or positions of authority, teaching to them a mantra so radically different, than perhaps what they knew growing up. Usually there is a chord or two of the mantra that hits a note of familiarity with the young person. In the gilded university setting, the young minds have what they believe to be is just short of an epiphany of truth. What they have truly had is a sweetly coated pill of radical ideology fed to them with a spoonful of sugar and wrapped nicely to make it look important.

Experts in marketing have cultivated for many years presentations to young adults to make their products not only appear attractive but come across as *must haves*. The goal is for what is offered, i.e. 'X, to be so enticing the young person believes his or her life will not be complete without 'X'. In the case of a radical ideology, they are taught their support of this specific agenda is not only good for them but for society as a whole. What is marketed, for example, as a compelling compassion for the poor and isolated in rough villages across Palestine is actually well dressed anti-Semitism and anti-Zionism all packaged in the caring for the young and elderly who cannot fend for themselves. The students or young adults do not necessarily grasp onto the ideology as a way of turning their back on Israel, but rather see themselves as championing the cause of the weak and the oppressed. They may even see society as the oppressor not individuals of the Jewish faith. They can form a dichotomy, in their minds, between support for the Palestinian people and the ruthless actions of those who rule with an iron fist over them.

Because of the Palestinian leadership, many Arabs are destined to live lives of poverty rather than those of prosperity that has come to thousands of Arabs who are citizens of Israel and working daily at careers they have enjoyed in relative comfort and peace. In fact, the only time their peace is disrupted is when their own leadership in Palestine attack places like the Ashkelon power plant which provides power to Israel and the West Bank. Searching for purpose, the young minds of today are being molded by some very unscrupulous people. It is time those of a good and worthwhile theology or even philosophy of life reach out to these young minds eager to soak up what they are taught and begin to teach them the truth of the situation in Israel and the Middle East. By remaining out of the fray, those of us who support Israel have abdicated the victory to the opponent without even entering the debate. There is little that now those so indoctrinated will hear but if the battle is not engaged, society and specifically Israel will lose and that is an untenable situation. The sleeper cells being placed across the U.S. today will someday awaken.

Is it within the bounds of propriety that we should argue for those in authority to keep watch over what is being taught by those affiliated with local universities? Certainly, there are those who would argue in quick denunciation of such a tactic as being unscrupulous to the extreme of being un-American, bordering on Fascist. There are those, too, who would argue such a knowledge is not enough but that such rancorous teachings should be quashed and driven from every corner of academic life. Sadly, then, there are those in the middle who would argue an *ends justifies the means* philosophy is not only tolerable in the stopping of a potential terrorist threat but that it is the only way to survive. There must be an argument that requires neither the denunciation of American values of freedom of speech nor does it demand a Marxist justification. The answer lies within at what point information gleaned though such a watchfulness ties to action. Is there enforcement action taken against some proponent of the ideology when there is no blatant call to violence? If so, that is an irrefutable violation of that for which America stands. Is there a creation of lists of people who subscribe to the ideology or who teach it without any demand being made by those persons to strike out against our society? If so, then, too, we have violated our own conscience for the sake of paranoia and we will be the less for it. Do not get my point wrong, however. There has always been, and must always be, within the bounds of good police work the watchful eye over those one believes may have the propensity to commit a criminal act with the goal being to stop such an act before it comes to fruition. It is what the initial belief is based upon that is the difference between good police work and the ghosts of Gestapo. This is not the place for a course in police ethics; but it is a course, if you will, in realism. HUMINT, or human intelligence, will always depend upon taking bits and pieces of information gleaned from shadowy places of gray that will someday be the piece of Intel which solves the crime much to the relief of the community and usually, the society will not want to know from where the information came or how it was obtained. Someone must keep their fingers on the pulse of those who might wish our nation ill. It is society's, and in most cases, the local community's responsibility to see to it that the finger is attached to someone of *high* convictions and not *multiple* ones.

Perhaps it is odd to place the discussion of tracking such threats as may be found in ideological expressions on college campuses in the midst of determining the Priority A, B and C resources within your community. However, it brings up a salient point that must be understood by all who would attempt to foresee any such attack. We must realize there are individuals within our midst who seek to destroy us. They shop with us, go to restaurants, municipal events, to work and to school with us. That realization should scare the beejeebers out of normally rationale people.

Thankfully most Americans are not normally rational people. When someone threatens our way of life, we usually get angry and want to take the fight to them rather than choose to be afraid. The ultimate goal of a terrorist is to make people so afraid of what *might happen* they abandon their normal way of life. I do not believe that terrorists will ever be able to achieve that goal with Americans. Just recently there was an article in a national news magazine that asked the question, *"Are We Losing the War Against Terror?"* I believe I made it clear earlier we are not engaged in a war against terror. We are engaged in a war against terrorists. There is a very large difference between the two.

To answer the implied question the author made, the answer is the Obama administration in Washington hampered our ability to make significant progress against the terrorists. What the Trump administration may do in the years ahead is unknown. Are we losing? The answer is, no. Americans will not lose the war against terrorists simply because Americans refuse to allow people like these terrorists to make us afraid; particularly afraid enough to abandon our lives as Americans. To the point, however, of watching and knowing who within our own communities may be advocating a terrorist attack against us, we in law enforcement and those involved in developing the intelligence, human and otherwise, must be very fastidious in the accuracy of this Intel.

The reality is that those exact same people who may end up on your version of a terrorist-watch list are also directly linked to one of your Priority A, B or C targets. If, in fact, such terrorist propaganda is being espoused on a college campus, it is very likely that campus is exactly where a sleeper-cell may hit. It could be from within that group that the sleeper awakens. It may be from a rival faction. It may be an attack on the school that has nothing whatsoever to do with their political machinations. This may be particularly true if a large percentage of the local economy is tied up with the university. Who, but the local community, would stand to lose the most if that school were shuttered by some horrific bomb blast which leveled a substantial amount of the university? As gruesome as such thoughts are, those are the types of thoughts the seasoned prognosticator must have.

The rankings of A, B, and C can be molded to the local need; but, a basic frame work will be most useful when working cross-jurisdictional boundaries. Primarily, the use of the three-letter system is designed to allow for a division between the most vital of local resources, the inclination being those most valued locally will also be those most targeted and therefore worthy of protection. From the enamored pages of the *Keep It Simple (insert adjective)* *Planning Guide* comes the concept that a single letter identification and a limit to three main priority resources is the most likely to get your agency and/or your community off the dime and doing some actual planning, preparation, prognostication, and prevention. To attempt to handle more than three primary resources at the outset is to overwhelm the planning staff because the number of variables will grow almost exponentially as the number of resources to protect increases.

Considering your community and its interaction with local universities, it is important to approach this special sub-community, if you will, carefully. The local university is a combination 'Priority Resource' and potential incubator of harmful individuals who are wrestling with the ideas espoused by community and family and those thrown at them by people presented to them as educated elders. It may be that certain of these elders seek to instigate violent acts across a generation. My own experiences from within university settings informs me that within the mindset of the faculty, trustees and alumni there is very often an inherent desire to do whatever it takes to protect the collective, the amorphous je ne se qua that is the university's life-force. In the science fiction story, Minority Report, the collective intelligence had to find a way to silence the mind that disputed the majority's finding for without that unanimity, the collective mind could not function. Protection of its position and power was critical to its survival and to allow dissention was to threaten its existence. The local student body must be careful not to adopt a similar mindset if the university has, in fact, evolved into such a being. The campus community has the capability of becoming everything to the student and even to the faculty and staff. When it does, protection of it can allow those so affected to go beyond rational bounds in helping the university to survive. When integral members of that community espouse rhetoric that leads the masses to believe that without the violence called for by

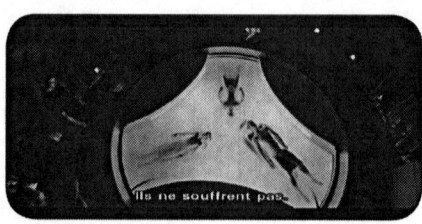

ideologues in support of their cause the university will no longer exist, regularly clear thinking persons can envision a loss of their most prized object; that university. When it is the minds of the masses that begin to do the thinking, normally sane individuals can find themselves lost in confusion it creates.

Another Hollywood generated example of such a similarity comes from the science fiction comedy, "Men in Black II". They are the 'Townspeople of Locker C18'[36]. They are content inside their bus station locker and have no desire to know there is something other than their own existence. No world outside their own truly exists or if it does, it is of little consequence to their daily world. The university community within the local community creates a conundrum that is a great place to begin stretching your *thin blue line*. It is true that the campus probably maintains their own campus police or security and you may be able to draw from them for typical personnel needs. But, to truly *stretch* this is the place where you recruit a member of the university faculty that understands well the mindset of the collective and can be educated to the needs of the local community and the threat that it faces. To do so is to find your first segment of your new line. This person would not work in a typical law enforcement function but he would be a liaison resource, and an information communicator (both directions) to and from the school and law enforcement. If a terrorist cell is building, he or she may be the first to suspect it, once they know whose ideology is being inculcated.

Others from the university world will be excellent stretchers to your line. Consider those on grounds and maintenance staffs. These people, particularly housekeepers, see and hear more than anyone. Often, they melt into the background and are the *gray* person we wrote of earlier. People talk in front of them because half of the time, no one even notices that they are there. They also have daily interactions with parts of the campus that will enable them to detect when something is not right. It may be a valve turned the wrong way or an acetylene torch sitting where it should not be. These are just a couple of any of a hundred plus scenarios. Even so, with all the planning and prevention, if an incident occurs at the university, these folks will be able to get you where you need to be and access to the equipment you need. These individuals are line stretchers. How you decide then to label the university in the A, B, or C priorities depends largely on whether there are other local resources more pressing. Often it is a matter of community-wide planning that brings these resources to the fore.

Priorities for Contingency Planning within the Geo-Spatial Aspects of the Community

In a recent paper, "Anticipating Urban Evacuations: A Planning Support System for Impact Reduction" written by Joshua Belhadj, MPA and published by the University of Cincinnati, certain basic principles of infrastructure planning were outlined which can be applied to the case made here. In his abstract, Belhadj wrote, "Today's world requires urban planners and researchers to explore terrorism possibilities as a new paradigm of disaster planning. Natural disaster planning can serve as a starting point for developing theories and models for understanding planning for man-made disasters, however, new practices are needed to encompass new unique characteristics."[37] The geo-spatial aspects of modern U.S. cities have the potential to positively influence the survival rate for local citizens in the event of an attack against the United States.

City planners must now consider the ways in which the basic municipal infra-structure can either hinder or promote evacuating citizens smoothly and safely when disasters strike, which may include homegrown or imported terrorist attacks. It need not be only terrorist attacks; but, planners should consider all probabilities for either natural or criminal events that require the immediate and mass evacuation of the maximum numbers of local citizens away from the hazardous zones. By contemplating and attempting to predict which areas of a community contain the highest level of priority resources and understanding individual community plans to facilitate such mass movement. Belhadj writes, "The main finding is that planners can use this framework to anticipate likely terrorism targets, and detect shortcomings in the city's building assets by analyzing indicators such as evacuee miles traveled, percent of evacuees traveling an unacceptable evacuation distance, and vulnerability of suspected targets."[38]However, as we brought to the fore in earlier pages, the local community has had little encouragement to consider the local implications of such attacks. It has fallen either to the federal government or often, if on a local level, to the actual operator of the resource site that is considered at risk. Belhadj writes, "A review of existing literature suggests that community level planning is not as savvy in anticipating man-made disasters and their resulting evacuations as it could be. There is a gap in the literature, where on the one hand, planning for terror is discussed at the federal level, and on the other hand discussed at a site-specific level. There is little research at the urban community level."[39] The September 11, 2001 attack on the Twin Towers added the visual impact that an attack on the Towers would have with the cultural message against western capitalism to

the geo-spatial aspect of an attack against an extremely crowded population center trapped on an island with only seven substantial bridges in the immediate vicinity. The logistics of just getting people out of downtown would be nearly impossible.[40]

The key component of what Belhadj writes indicates that without first determining the highest priority of resources which could become a major terrorist target, it is not possible to accurately plan the geo-spatial resources necessary for a mass exodus of citizens. The planners within the community context whether employed directly by the municipality or professional planners employed by research and planning firms are very much the types of persons the local law enforcement planners should include in the new fiber of the **Blue Line.** Belhadj is primarily concerned with the evacuation of persons from a city *after* a terrorist attack. That is a fine and appropriate goal. His techniques, however, utilize some of the same planning and forecasting scenarios that must be considered if law enforcement and all those affiliated with its mission to *serve and protect* are to eliminate the need for an evacuation. That is accomplished by stopping or preventing the terrorist attack in the first place.

Where Belhadj takes the intelligence determinates of high priority resources and determines an action plan for *what if* a terrorist attacks, what is proposed here is that those same determinates can facilitate the protection of the priority resources and the interdiction of the terrorists *before* the attack can take place. The primary starting point must be at the identification of priority resources. The government has begun with a formula designed to help work all of that part out. At some points in the documents written by the federal government it appears that *their experts* have come to grasp every known issue without fail. Perhaps it is the nature of the organization to see itself in the best light, a tendency any of us would do well to avoid for the sake of those depending upon our pre-planning to help keep them clear of the present danger.

Consider the following passage Mr. Belhadj writes regarding the role of the DHS in the current scenarios for preventing terrorists seeking to destroy local resources. "The Department of Homeland Security has initiated the Risk Analysis and Management of Critical Asset Protection (RAMCAP) project as an attempt to capitalize on and integrate private sector knowledge and expertise with government information and resources." Perhaps it might be more aptly named the Risk Analysis and Management of Critical Resources and Asset Protection. Then we can understand that *RAMCRAP's* purpose is to first take all the information possible from the private sector and then classify the results so the private sector cannot access them. At least it has a more appropriate acronym. In the process of doing just that the DHS will screen what they determine to be high priority infrastructure resources to determine which ones cross "at-risk" and "significance to the nation" thresholds as outlined by *their program* guidelines. The result is a classified database of nationally critical infrastructures called the National Asset Database (NADB) that aids allocation of federal risk management resources.

It is important to critically dissect the federal government's (DHS's) strategy. First, they created a program with an acronym. Both, (a program and an acronym), are vital to obtaining federal dollars. Next, they, (that is DHS), are prepared to create a list of priority resources that are deemed *significant to the nation*. Then, the DHS will gather information from civilian experts on the resources *they believe* to be *at risk*. The matrix created will yield a section of data where the two fields (significant and at risk) intersect. Circle A is what the DHS deems to be nationally important and Circle B is what their civilian experts deem to be at risk. The shaded area C is what makes the database.

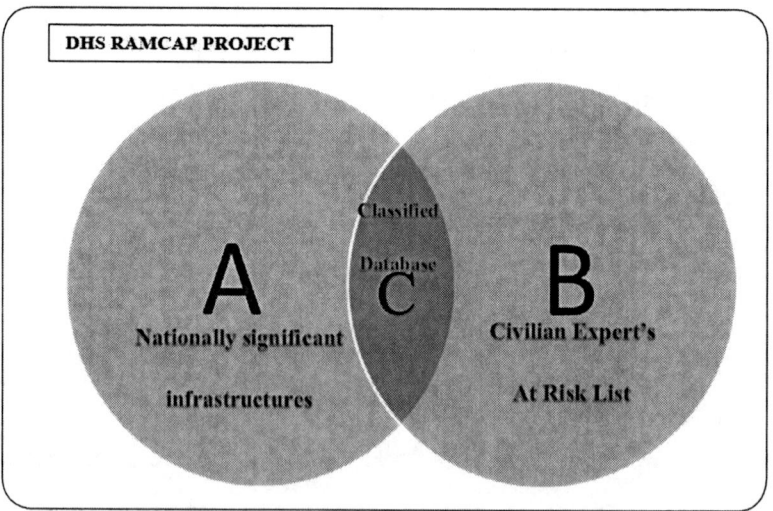

Those resources then are identified as *nationally critical infra-structures*. Those identified *nci's* are placed on a list titled National Asset Database. The database is then "CLASSIFIED." *That means that the DHS will determine who gets to see the list.* The purpose of the database is to 'aid in the allocation of federal resources.' If the problems with such a federal program are not immediately evident then please allow a few moments of review. First, it is a federal program run by folks in Washington. Remember at the outset, I made the point that, 'the best holder of the reins is the one who must ride the horse…it is their own arse that is up there in the saddle.' Simply stated: when the federal government decides which resources should be on the priority list, it will be only those *they determine* to have *significance to the nation.* That may be understandable at the 30,000 feet viewpoint of Washington D.C. planners. At ground level, where the average citizen must live and work, the local elementary school's first grade class with 27 children in it does not rank for the DHS like it does for local law enforcement and the community. You can bet Miss Green's First Grade Class is a priority resource to the community and locally they will set about plans to protect it. You *cannot* count on the feds to do that for you. It is not their job. *It is yours.* The feds are dealing with *nationally significant infrastructures – only.*

The key component of what Belhadj writes indicates that without first determining the highest priority of resources that could become a major terrorist target, it is not possible to accurately plan the geo-spatial resources necessary for a mass exodus of citizens. The planners within the community context whether employed directly by the municipality or professional planners employed by research and planning firms are very much the types of persons the local law enforcement planners should include in the new fiber of the **Blue Line.**

Note a second issue with the RAMCRAP program the DHS is putting together. *They* choose the experts to gather *their* infrastructure information with the specifications *they* require. Who knows more about the side door that is always propped open at the NE corner of the chemical plant off Water Street in your town? An expert on Chemical Engineering from MIT or Joe, the man who has handled the maintenance and janitorial duties by himself for over fifteen years at the chemical plant? Which do you want to be part of stretching your local 'thin blue line?' Do you need to know the chemical properties the engineer provides if things go wrong? Absolutely! At least in the context of first responder safety and long term deleterious effects. Is his information pertinent to battling the blaze once it is ignited? Absolutely! But here we are trying to stop the attack *before* it happens and in this framework, we need Joe *first.*

A third point on the DHS plan, and then I'll stop there because this could go on *ad nauseum* if I'm not careful. This point has to do with federal assistance. I said it was one point but, still, I have to make it a two-part point. The purpose of the list according to DHS is to *aid in the allocation of federal resources.* Replace 'resources' with 'money' and you see that you only get money or federal help if your resource (that has made their list) has just been blown to bits by an al Qaeda (or some other presidentially defined as *non-religious Islamic extremist*) sleeper cell who just woke up in your home town. The other part is the database itself. As I mentioned briefly before, the database with all those priority resources which we must be ready to protect is *classified.* That simply means no one will ever know what resources are on that list until after it has been blown up by Ahmed Sertaperfectsleeper and Congress authorizes dollars to be spent to rebuild whatever infrastructure it was… By the way, you did notice that to be on the list the resource had to be *infrastructure.*

Thankfully, Mr. Belhadj recognizes the folly here in depending on the federal government to protect local resources, especially if they are going to use the DHS's *RAMCRAP* project. The federal government is not designed to handle local issues. Terrorists can be stopped at the local level, as we have noted, because pulling off an attack requires pre-planning which requires on-site activity which also requires obtaining materials. During all this pre-planning, the risk of being observed is extremely high. Local citizens who are aware, working with local law enforcement can be the ones to make the report that stops an attack before it happens.

Working hand-in-hand with a team of infra-structure experts will provide the law enforcement planners with both additional expertise in project planning, procurement of materials, development of construction teams and implementation of the action plans necessary for upgrading the current bridges, local roads and expressways that make-up the current infra-structure. Working directly with these planners, local law enforcement officials will be able to comprehend more clearly the ways in which the up-grading of the infra-structure will help the overall assessment of the vulnerabilities of those resources that are infra-structure specific. Additional methodologies will be necessary for determining the vulnerabilities of those resources which are not infra-structure related. Local officials must understand their purview is *all local assets* which include much more than infrastructure, particularly infrastructure that is nationally significant. Officials on the local level must also acknowledge they cannot expect federal assistance on non-nationally significant resources.

ASSESSING THE VULNERABILITIES OF PRIORITIES

The first team developed under the local law enforcement's *New Centurion* program should be a Priority Assessment Team. Its role is to review the committee's fairly exhaustive list of priorities. Working together, the committee and Priority Assessment Team (C-PAT) begins to whittle the list down in search of a workable group of Priority A, B, and C designees. The Priority Assessment Team's objective is to assess the risk to each of them. It may be helpful, as a whittling tool, to create a list of several resources under each category. Each may include ten to twelve resources under 'A' and like numbers under 'B' and 'C'.

Then it may be more feasible to prioritize those down to a maximum of three under each category.

It is also helpful for the C-PAT to categorize each of the three priorities by types. That is: Priority A may be 'human targets'; Priority B infrastructure targets; Priority C military or weapons type targets which might include local gun dealers or manufacturers. The types can be fashioned along with each communities' needs. For example, if there are no military bases or weapons capabilities within the area that designation may be used for 'educational targets' or another type target more in line with the local community resources. The committee can make determinations whether a location like a hospital may be in the 'human' category A or a separate category under healthcare/healthcare-research. Once this highly complex and perhaps time-consuming part of the evaluation is completed; it is then the time for determining the risk values.

In my initial writings on risk assessment and the management of those risks, I utilized a four by four and at times a five by five matrix to review the risks that specific assets may be under. As we review that matrix, it is important to understand that the purpose of the matrix was not to set a fixed forecast in stone of the risks and their vulnerabilities and leave it at that. Rather, the matrices described below are designed to become a living document that monitors the movement of the level of risk over time as variables impact the risk level.

In both the four by four and five by five risk assessment tool the vertical and horizontal axis are: *intensity of impact* on the community, company, team or even nation and the *probability of the event* respectively. The intensity of impact is rated on a 1 to 4, or 1 to 5 on the secondary example, with the higher the number the more critical the impact of the risk. The highest number indicates an impact so critical that the unit for which it is measuring (team, country etc.) will cease to exist or function for the foreseeable future.

The horizontal axis, which indicates the probability of the event happening, is on a matching scale of one to four or one to five. The higher the number the more likely the event will take place. A four or five, respectfully, indicates an imminence of the event. If, then, there is a risk that is both a five on the level of critical impact and a five on the probability of an attack which is imminent, it is time to find a place for shelter until the worst is past. If you cannot become a turtle with a ballistic protective shell, then it is time to find the closest proximal shelter.

On a side note, according to the military and others who have utilized this ranking, the primary reason for delineating on a five rather than a four chart is out of a need for more detailed levels of movement between the stages of risk based on the variables that impact each. If a finer demarcation is needed, then the five scale is more conducive to a plainly read chart. The following example is created for determining risk patterns of natural disasters.

RISK ANALYSIS MATRIX: NATURAL DISASTER (hurricane, flood, etc.)					
		1	2	3	4	5
Immanent	5					
Expected	4					
Probable	3					
Likely	2					
Very Unlikely	1					
		Minimal Loss damage minor low cost repair operations continue without interruption	Moderate Loss Costs manageable operations. continue with 1 week	Serious Loss Cost of repair high but operations continue with two – three. week interruption	Major Loss Months to restart	Total Loss unable to continue operations

In the primary use of the risk analyses described above, the risks for which they are designed are: Natural (weather related disasters), Political (coup, etc.), and Medical (pandemic, epidemic etc.), and Criminal (terrorism).[41] A separate matrix is developed for each risk that is being evaluated. As time passes and intelligence reports provide information on the likelihood of the events coming to pass, such as movement along a fault line in anticipation of an earthquake, the ranking increases. As intelligence indicates that a terrorist cell has obtained a nuclear device capable of killing multitudes of Americans, as China's recent boast of a ship-fired nuclear device that can strike the west coast of the United States killing between five and fifteen thousand persons[42], the impact ranking of the risk increases. Similar evaluation matrices and formulas are being developed to fine tune the prognostications of both governmental and private agencies.

The U.S. Department of Homeland Security's *National Infrastructure Protection Plan* utilizes a formulation designed to create the factor of risk valuation. The formulation makes it possible to assign a value to each of a specific number of variables. The compilation of those values will provide an overall value for the individual resource. Once that risk value is determined then action can follow based on informed priority rankings. The process is shown in the following chart.

Risk Where:	= f(Consequence, Vulnerability, Threat)
Risk	= expected loss
Consequence	= the resulting death, destruction, devastation brought by a completed attack
Vulnerability	= the degree to which the resource is unprotected or unable to be protected from the threat
Threat	= probability of being attacked

The DHS formulation is based on the Environmental Research Institute's 2006 formulation for determining a level of impact.

Their formula is shown in the next chart.

Risk Where:	
Risk	= the expected outcome of an attack
Impact of Loss	= the worst-case possible negative effects of an attack, given that an attack occurs
Vulnerability	= degree to which the subject is vulnerable to attack, given that an attack occurs

Under the Department of Homeland Security's NIPP protocol there are three objectives that are underscored by the risk analysis. Those three are: "**deter threats, mitigate vulnerabilities, and minimize consequence.**"[43]

The most difficult aspect of the process is to determine which of the resources being evaluated are possibly at risk for a sleeper cell type of attack. Since knowing, as a certainty what resources are most targeted without the HUMINT to back up the intelligence is improbable, it is necessary to consider every resource as the most likely to be the target. When the community's Priority Assessment Team evaluates the resources that have made it to the *priority list* they must decide where to focus their limited protection resources. One methodology for determining where to place those resources is to find those which are the most vulnerable to attack. The vulnerability of a resource is defined under the DHS format: *the degree to which the resource is unprotected or unable to be protected from the threat.* When using the formula method, it is necessary to assign a value to the level of each variable.

There is an issue that comes with the 5x5 scale or similar model used by the military and DHS. The issue is two-fold. Either the assigning of the 1 to 5 ranking is too subjective and your 4 is someone else's 3 or the definitions for each value are so complicated the entire analysis sits on the shelf and is never used. I am recommending that following the 3 goals listed by DHS which, you recall are: deter threats, mitigate vulnerabilities, and minimize consequences, we will simplify the risk rankings as **LOW, MEDIUM and HIGH.** This ranking system takes into account the subjectivity that can come during the ranking process and it eliminates the burdensome definitions for each numerical score. It is not a stretch to say that intuitively people working within this field understand in fairly consistent terms when a colleague is using terminology of Low Risk, Medium Risk and High Risk.

Using this simplified scale, if a resource is determined to be a high-level target of the terrorists then the threat 't' ranking of HIGH. If both the consequence 'c' rankings and the vulnerability 'v' rankings are also HIGH, then not surprisingly the aggregate score or risk factor for that resource is HIGH. Understanding how elementary that example sounds, let's simply complicate it just a bit and make it more *real world.* You know that if a resource is already HIGH in every category, you don't have to call a group meeting to determine that it is necessary to allocate resources there. You will want to accelerate your intelligence gathering on the target. But what if the values are not three lemons straight across the screen?

If the evaluation of a resource shows you its 't' ranking is HIGH plus if it were taken out the consequences or 'c' ranking is MEDIUM, (perhaps because of its limited community impact or remote location) and because of previous security emphasis its 'v' ranking is LOW then what is your composite? When out of three rankings you get a HIGH, MEDIUM and LOW does the aggregate or composite 'c' ranking equal MEDIUM? The answer in the real world is *yes* and *no*.

In the example given the 't' ranking was HIGH. When the threat level is HIGH that trumps all other rankings. A 't' of HIGH equals an overall score of HIGH. If you have Humint or other intelligence which says the enemy is coming for this one, no matter how big or little the consequences and no matter how currently vulnerable it is– the ranking is HIGH because when the enemy gets there to take it– you better be there ahead of him! If other rankings come in HIGH, MEDIUM and LOW, as long as it is not the 't' ranking that is HIGH then the composite score of MEDIUM is applied.

The higher the 'r' value is for a local priority resource the more attention it will receive from those responsible for resource protection. One contingency action will be to harden the target and make it less vulnerable. Recall one of the stated objectives was to *deter an attack*. It will be shown making a resource less vulnerable is a deterrence to attack.

The Priority Assessment Team may determine it is advantageous to assign specific roles to other teams. A Resource Protection Team will review the specific vulnerabilities and take whatever actions are necessary to mitigate the lapses in its security. The Consequence Reduction Team could be responsible for developing ways to mitigate the damage both direct and collateral inflicted by an attack. Part of their work may be to include the information provided by those like Mr. Belhadj to facilitate the rapid evacuation of persons from the impact area and thus lowering the consequences of the event. The focus of the Consequence Reduction Team will always assume a completed aggressive act. It may seek to formulate separate strategies based on varying degrees of 'successes' of the attacker(s).

The Threat Intelligence Team will be the one most directly connected to information sources which are local, state, federal and international in scope. They will be gleaning information from intelligence reports and a multiplicity of sources to attempt to determine the likelihood of an attack anywhere in the U.S. and at times anywhere in the world when intel on an upcoming attack is very vague. Once the intelligence is becoming more target specific the Threat Intelligence Team will be able to either upgrade or downgrade a resource's 't' factor.

It is appropriate for the *New Centurions* to develop a response strategy based on both the aggregate score of local targeted resources and on an upgrade in the 'r' rating of a resource. Next, we shall investigate whether it may be possible to determine the enemy's target selection based on a resource's 'v' rating.

CAN ASSETS BE TARGETED BY THEIR VULNERABILITIES?

In the previous section, it was understood that most often the 'r' value of a resource was contingent upon the value placed on the resource by the enemy, whoever that may be, by whatever standard they might use (i.e. western debauchery, financial impact or human life) as well as the function of the inter-related variables of consequence, vulnerability and threat. Recall the variable *threat* 't' is defined for our purposes here as: the probability of being attacked. We know increasing the values of 'c', 'v', and 't' increase the 'r' value or the risk of a target being attacked. But can a resource become a target simply based on its 'v' value? If so, how can that 'v' value be lowered to remove the resource from the high-risk category?

The burgeoning Thin Blue Line now should find itself equipped with *experts* from a variety of sources from university fellows to night janitorial staffers, tactical response experts to covert intelligence analysts, realtors to social media surfers and, yes, even community planners. There will be a plethora of opinions which may become obstructive if not properly directed. Those opinions can also most certainly be illuminating when the darkness seems about to overtake the entire process. Fresh life breathed into the team from within its own framework can enliven the group, particularly when it is more comfortable to claim a hearty 'well-done' and *'let's do this again in another lustrum or two.'*

Perhaps the most difficult aspect of this entire endeavor is the highest pinnacle of success of the process comes from there never being even a hint at an attempted attack. The teams may never know whether any terrorist had ever looked their way and been thwarted by their efforts. Rather, life will go on in a hum-drum existence without the blaring claxon call to arms when the enemy is at the gate. Quiet and still will be the night that most who worked to keep it so will not know if evil ever lurked in the shadows.

To maintain a commitment to the task, which can at times be tedious and unheralded, the team leaders must inspire the teams to a watch completed without so much of a tear shed because of some nefarious act against their community. To create such a success requires, as we said at the beginning, a reliance on the Divine and a commitment of this service to Him. With that must be, too, the on-going re-evaluation of resources and their 'r' values. The question is posed as to whether the 't' value of a resource can be determined by its 'v' value. Certainly the 'r' value is influenced to a great degree by 'v' but can 'v' determine 't'? This is more than an exercise in shuffling *Shinola*[44]. We know if we lower any value (HIGH to MEDIUM etc.) among the variables the overall 'r' value goes down and the safety of the resource is considered, at least, more secure. But, is it possible to lessen the enemies' attraction to a resource so much so by reducing its 'v' rating it will turn away suicidal driven religious fanatics from attempting to gain access at all? I believe if a resource carries a 'c' value that is LOW and its vulnerability is also LOW, it becomes a non-starter for the enemy. When that happens, it will be completely removed from the enemies' target list. The 'v' ranking may not *determine* 't' but it can certainly *impact* it.

The concept is simple in theory. If a resource (target) is hardened to the point the vulnerability of it is as near zero as can be had in the real world, even the most proficient terrorist will by-pass it for more vulnerable targets. This is true, I believe, for two reasons both of which are based on contemplating the machinations of criminal minds and observing criminal behavior for over forty years. Their decision to by-pass a properly hardened target will be based on one of two motivations. The first is laziness. The second is efficiency. The less professional of the criminal or terrorist the lazier they are. They will by-pass a hardened target for a more vulnerable target simply because it is easier to accomplish.

The latter example is the more professional criminal or terrorist. He or she does not by-pass a hardened target out of laziness but out of serious calculations. He or she considers the amount of time and expense required to execute the plan at target hardened '#1' versus accomplishing the same amount of terror, destruction, death and mayhem at more vulnerable target '#2' with much less expense in time and effort, even money. That is not even to add into the equation and thought process about the risk of being captured or killed. It is true this expectation may not be applicable to the crazed zealot, however. There may be one aspect of the hardened target that so enthralls him or so captivates his thinking he cannot pass on this one target. It might be in the name of the facility or a staff member there for which he holds a particular grudge. He may look forward to a martyr's death that is assured by the hardened defenses.

As in most planning processes, the deranged mind can be so incredibly unpredictable. Still, a sufficiently hardened target, can help to determine the probability of it being targeted and reduce its 't' value and a sufficiently low 'v' value can impact its 't' value. If it is properly hardened, should the zealot make his attempt, he will be stopped before any innocent blood is shed. That, too, is a victory for the Centurions.

The reverse of this process is also applicable, particularly in the United States. I make this claim also based on over a dozen years of experience in working cross-culturally in high-risk areas overseas. One area in particular provides an excellent example of this point. Israel, a nation under attack by its neighbors since its rebirth in 1948, has come to understand the necessity for target hardening and the civilian's role in assisting in maintaining a hard target structure. Israeli soldiers, which includes every Israeli citizen at some point in their life with but a few exceptions for religious or physical reasons, all carry weapons. In the U.S. military, for example, only certain specialties carry weapons, most do not. For those that do, none carry weapons when they are 'off-duty'. If they had, the mass murders by an Islamic cleric in a soldier's chaplain uniform would not have been successful at Fort Hood Texas recently.

In the IDF every soldier carries a weapon and no soldier is ever truly off-duty. So, in the local grocery store not only will you see soldiers in uniform carry fully automatic weapons slung over their shoulder but the young lady working the cash register in civilian clothes may also be a soldier and she will also have an automatic weapon on her shoulder.

In Israel, students, faculty and staff at Jerusalem University, park their cars on the perimeter of the school and walk onto campus. Every single person goes through the same screening as Americans now must go through in airports. Going into the local market or shopping plaza, every person will go through a metal detector and have their purse or whatever satchel they might be carrying searched by a heavily armed guard. Even the YMCA has two armed guards at the doorway allowing only guests into the building and continually under electronic, and often personal, surveillance. One does not simply enter a hospital and stroll up to the floor to visit a sick friend. Hardened security awaits the civilian at every corner. It is a fact of their life and they are more than quite comfortable with this reality.

America has not been under the continual threats and attacks Israel has been. America, too, is exponentially larger than Israel. An attack in New York City does not impact citizens in Los Angeles like an attack in Tel Aviv affects citizens in Jerusalem. It is easier for Americans to disassociate what is going on in one area of the country and so their perception of the threat for them personally is less. They are then less likely to accept having to stand in line to go through a metal detector to enter their local shopping mall. Americans are so intractable in this regard the hardening of certain resources in the United States is unlikely. An alternative exists, however, in the individual freedom Americans have to carry firearms and in many states, under certain conditions, to carry them concealed. The Second Amendment to the United States Constitution says it well. "A well-regulated Militia being necessary to the security of a Free State, the right of the people to keep and bear arms shall not be infringed."[45]

With the general spirit of Americans to forego what they believe to be excessive restriction of their freedom of movement by the implementation of safeguards such as Israel has in place, until such time the threats have become real enough that obstinacy to the security measures is reduced, the best alternative response in the U.S. is that properly trained, reputable citizens take the responsibility to carry a firearm for the defense of themselves and others. That in and of itself may prove to be enough of a deterrent in some regards to eliminate part of the threat. There is a quote attributed to Admiral Yamamoto of Japan which is at this point unsubstantiated but the quote goes, "You cannot invade the United States, there would be a rifle behind every blade of grass."[46]

The deterrence factor of such an impression of the United States is perhaps more necessary today than in WWII. Our attackers today are more likely to be one or two lone wolf sleeper cells who are attempting to spread terror through random appearing acts of violence. They will be more easily stopped by an average American carrying a concealed firearm and, I believe, more easily dissuaded from their mission if they believe that as they look across a group of American citizens at least one in ten of those citizens has a firearm and is trained in its use. The actual numbers vary based on the source but an average of 50 percent of Americans own firearms and about 7% are licensed to carry a concealed firearm and in some states, there is no requirement for a license to carry a concealed firearm.[47] Not bad propaganda to spread really. That brings us to the question as to whether Citizen Centurions can protect America's resources.

CAN CITIZEN CENTURIONS FILL THE NEED TO PROTECT THOSE ASSETS?

Citizen Centurions cannot protect local assets from *Terrorism*. Did you read that correctly? Perhaps it should be re-stated another way. *Citizen Centurions* cannot protect local assets from an ambiguous, nebulous, and formless methodology of warfare. That is one reason why the *War on Terror* has never been an effective mentality. No more than all the soldiers of the Polish Army were able to defeat *the blitzkrieg* can American citizens and local law enforcement defeat *terrorism*. As first treated in 'Defining the Threat in Human Terms' in Section 2.3, the principle of putting a human face on a nebulous enemy can only improve the ability of the defender to turn the game to one of offense and successfully remove the threat. A single Polish soldier can effectively take-out a tank commander. A squad of Polish soldiers could take out the command and control unit for a strategic field artillery unit. The tank commander is an individual soldier. The command and control unit is made up of human beings who are soldiers. The concept is clear. When Polish soldiers as individuals or as combat units had an accurately defined target that had human structure, which had the possibility to make errors and required the inhalation of O_2 and exhalation of CO_2 then those individuals who utilized *blitzkrieg* as a methodology of war could be defeated.

Citizen Centurions and local law enforcement cannot defeat *terrorism*. They can, however, defeat *terrorists* who are individuals that work alone or in coordinated groups, who have the propensity to make mistakes, and require both the inhalation of O_2 and exhalation of CO_2. Americans do not do themselves or their warriors any favors by elevating these often-incompetent foot soldiers to a mystical level of worldwide fear. They are fallible human beings and American cops and the citizens they serve can educate themselves, train and prepare to do more than just engage the enemy. They can develop the skill set necessary for eliminating the individuals who bring the threat of death and fear to their communities and neighborhoods. The time to go on offense is now and the tools to do so are within the grasp of local authorities.

Chapter 3

Locally Owned

Transition of Power

America is at cross-roads. There comes a time within any government and particularly within a democracy to re-evaluate the game plans used thus far. If the *game* and being *on the offense* analogy is taken further, then there is a time for those to take the field who have been warming the bench the entire game. They were benchwarmers only because the *first string* upper classmen desired only to win their precious 'letters' regardless of their true capabilities. There are men and women who have been drawing up fresh new game plans designed for use by the *second stringers* who fit their capabilities and match the needs of the game when the clock is in the final minutes.

Those currently in the halls of Congress and stalking the halls of the White House would consider themselves the upper classmen who must dominate every phase of the game. Their campaign managers and media hucksters have been running the agendas and calling the plays rather than men and women who are dedicated only to the growth and strength of the American people, by which America itself is made strong. Those currently in power have as a goal only to grow and strengthen themselves and their power base, which to them *is* America. The American citizens to them are inept and unaware; sheep in need of a shepherd. By keeping themselves in power they seek to find ways to keep the people dependent upon their handouts and social programs. Feeding the public the Pablum of policies keeps those citizens just weak enough to follow.

When an artist takes to his easel to draw some magnified view of life, a grand expression of the desires within himself he picks up the brush that is best for the image he is about to draw. Now comes a time to re-draw the Thin Blue Line.

RE-DRAWING THE THIN BLUE LINE

In one of 'God's coincidences' just as this section was about to be written, an amazing thunderstorm came barreling through our part of Ohio. A wall cloud was directly over our location. My son was able to snap this picture with his phone's camera. I share with you here a terrific display of the Thin Blue Line. There was in this instant just that thin blue line between the earth below and the fierce and violent maelstrom overhead.

It is time to re-draw the Thin Blue Line. "For the public, a thin blue line is all that exists between order and disorder and between civilization and anarchy. The police are the thin blue line."[49] A professor from Frostburg State University in Maryland made an interesting analogy between environmentalists and law enforcement first in their role as protectors but particularly from the standpoint that those who enforce laws without the ability to educate the public on the purpose and worthiness of the laws which are being enforced faces the possibility of promoting laws for the sake of obedience, even blind obedience. The laws have an effectiveness near zero because either the laws are not understood by the public, so they are thwarted at every turn; or the laws have continued for so long without an appropriate evaluation of their purpose they have, by outliving their purpose, made themselves useless.

A clear analysis of the threat, a succinct statement that defines success in this *war against terrorists on the local level,* an operation plan which takes into account every known fact gleaned from the risk analyses, and a census of the personnel needed to effectively execute the battle strategy are each vital to mission success. It is not the fate of the *Polposipus herculeanus*[50] that rests in the outcome of the battles to be fought in this war that is raging. It about the threatened extinction of that small parasitic beetle that lives in dead trees on a remote set of islands the Frostburg professor was writing. The analogy the professor made ends there because the thin blue line we hold has a much larger impact for civilization than the life of an insect. If the terrorists who are plotting a global annihilation of every person who chooses *not* to take up the terrorists' god should be victorious; then the fate of a beetle living in dead trees on the Isle of Seychelles will be of little consequence.   51

General Colin Powell has been praised and ridiculed for his enumeration of what has been called The Powell Doctrine on the considerations that must be given prior to the commitment of U.S. military resources and troops to a combat role *overseas*. If anything, after the Iraq War, much of what was presented in the Powell Doctrine was seen as having been set aside for the goals of the war whether those be military or political. One factor that has been brought out and it is crucial to remember: *The Powell Doctrine referred to the commitment of combat troops overseas not*

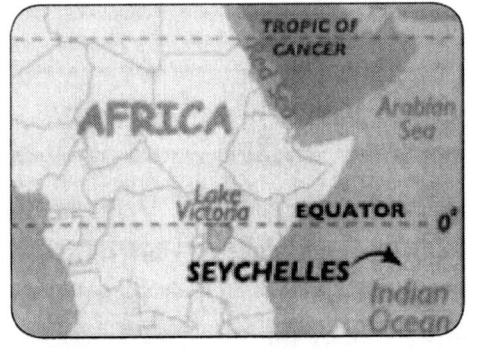

at home protecting the homeland. Here we will take the context of the Powell Doctrine with regard to having a clear strategy both for engagement and for a successful exit and apply it to a defense of the homeland by local law enforcement and those who have stepped into the breach to reinforce the thin blue line.   Michael Cohen wrote that the essence of the Powell Doctrine could be summed up as: "The United States must prepare for the conflicts that are not only in the country's vital interests, but that it can also bring to a satisfactory conclusion."[52] It is the latter half of this two-part *sine qua non* for engagement of the Thin Blue Line against those who would directly attack our communities that brings us to the deployment strategies for *the line* based on the *R*-ranking of each asset that stands in harm's way.

Deploying Troops Based on 'R' Rankings

Earlier in this text when first explaining the use of 'R' 'V' 'T' and 'C' rankings. The 'R' ranking is the *RISK* a particular asset or groups of assets may be facing either all in one community or in a broad attack upon several communities perhaps involving several assets in disparate locations. Included in the 'R' ranking is the ability of a community to, on its own, present the necessary resources to protect a high-risk asset for any length of time. The local capability greatly diminishes after 72 hours. That ability begins to decline the minute the clock starts to tick. If the Intel that is predicting a strike against an asset is crystal clear, highly sourced, specific to date, time and location you can be pretty sure it is a fraud; perhaps even a trap set to lure you in and strike either against your forces or on some other asset from which resources have been diverted.

Is it possible to utilize the Risk Ranking of a priority asset to determine the extent to which protection should be provided? This could be in the amount of discretionary funds that are applied to an asset as compared to other assets under the jurisdiction of the law enforcement agency. It may also be used to determine the numbers of personnel assigned to a protection detail. It should be noted these numbers are not static but extremely fluid based on the intelligence available on a particular asset that leads the planners to believe that this particular asset is being targeted at a specific point in time. It is important to understand as well that an asset's priority or its 'R' Ranking may be partly determined by its location. An example is found at the Mexico and U.S. border where at particular times, certain border crossings are more likely to be targeted by our enemies, such as ISIS to send would-be terrorist homicide bombers across the border and into America.

Authorities estimate that some 40,000 children and teens will cross the border from Mexico into the U.S. in 2015. "In just the first six months of the 2015 fiscal year, authorities report having apprehended 15,647 children crossing the border without parents. Many of them are teenagers from Central America.[53] Sheriff Paul Babeu of Pinal County Arizona reports on the impact such an influx of illegals has on U.S. border towns and his concern for further problems related to terrorism because of the border issues. The situation in the border towns is "bordering on flat out chaos." He also worries what the lack of border enforcement may signal to America's enemies... He cites a recent Judicial Watch report that indicates Islamic militants having a staging camp close to the U.S. border. One base is reportedly just a few miles from El Paso, Texas in an area known as 'Anapra' just west of Ciudad Juarez. A second cell is reportedly stationed in Puerto Palomas, another border town.... 'America's enemies see the weakness at our border... my fear is that it will take something catastrophic to happen before Washington and the Obama administration wake up and see the magnitude of the situation we are facing.'" Now that Pres. Trump is moving forward in hardening borders, we will see of the political winds change.

If you were the chief law enforcement officer for El Paso, Texas assuming that the issue of having a terrorist staging camp just across the border along with a continuing influx of illegal immigrants have made your border crossing onto your list of assets that rate a protective detail, how might you begin to determine the best course of action? Under the proposed analysis that we have outlined here it is necessary to determine the 'R' Ranking of the border crossing by utilizing the formula: *f(Consequence, Vulnerability, Threat)* and assign rankings for the Vulnerability 'V'- *the degree to which the resource is unprotected or unable to be protected from the threat* of the crossing, the 'T' or Threat Ranking *the probability of being attacked* and the Consequences or 'C' Ranking *the resulting death, destruction, devastation brought by a completed attack* for the border crossing.

Professor Kauffman of Frostburg University writes, "Looking at the earth from the outer reaches of the atmosphere, the atmosphere encircling the earth makes a thin blue line of life. To know, to educate and to protect the thin blue line and the life that it contains is the mission of the environmentalist. For the survival of the earth and it inhabitants, there is no more important mission than this."[54] As with many professions, among environmentalists there are those who truly devote themselves to pure science minus the politics for the sake of their role as protectors of earth. Much maligned for those of the fringe, true environmentalists seek to serve and protect. They cannot do so without the public. The same is true for law enforcement. Local law enforcement officers (LEOs) must have the assistance of the public they serve. Sometimes even that is not enough. Sometimes even the *homegrown needs help.*

With great candor and upon the heels of deep introspection, I confess if there is one aspect of the radical Islamic mindset which is much stronger than the average American's it is their unfettered willingness to do whatever it takes to win. Their resolve comes from a religious fervor. That fervor is real, although based on a fictional belief of a decadent afterlife with all the sexual gratification they were denied here on earth. The Prophet, though being very capricious, makes certain there is never any *real* guarantee of heaven and virgins; but, for the faithful committing what they believe to be a martyr's suicide is their best shot. (*Pun intended*). So, whether it is their zeal to gain heaven or their fear to avoid hell; it becomes a driving factor in their zeal. Such men and women, so driven, are difficult to defeat. They are not impossible to defeat, just difficult.

REDEPLOYING THE TROOPS BASED ON 'R' RANKINGS

Recently, I read a quip on a social media site that went something like this: *Well another day is done and I did not use Algebra even once.* The statement brings a smile to most of the faces of folks who struggled at one time in their life with freshman Algebra but it is not entirely a true statement because such mathematical operations are in play all around. The determination of the 'R' Ranking of a local resource has such an operation written into it. The goal here to understand how to deploy or redeploy your available law enforcement resources for the protection of these vital targets is best achieved by the use of a hypothetical example.

Earlier, the Professional Football Hall of Fame was mentioned as a particularly well attended tourist attraction in Northeast Ohio, particularly during the enshrinement ceremonies, vast parade festivities and pre-season professional football game all hosted in the relatively small town of Canton, Ohio. National and international media attention has its sights for the sports world on the Hall of Fame during that one week each August when old and new players alike mingle with thousands of fans at local festivities. Let us assume for this exercise you are the local law enforcement official who has been tasked with keeping these events, and particularly the enshrinement event, safe. You have taken the advice herein and brought together a stretched blue line that includes personnel from the NFL, the Hall of Fame, the local parade officials and even neighbors living in close proximity to the Hall of Fame who see traffic come and go at all hours of the night even when the *Hall* is closed. Now you must determine how best to use your thinly stretched resources for this particular event.

It is not possible to go into a deep analysis of all the contingencies which would need to be considered for the Hall of Fame. One simple aspect that is easy to decide, but difficult to implement, is the separation of the parade participants from the spectators. With the Boston Marathon as a history lesson, one can easily see how greater security is beneficial. How do you incorporate this into a community culture that has had the spectators and the parade participants within a few feet of each other and the ability to almost shake hands with them as they go by as the history? How do you drastically alter the parade into a physically secure environment? The streets themselves and the areas along which the parade route travels make such security almost impossible without a large expense in infrastructure changes. Redeploying troops along the parade route based on the 'R' Rating of the event is feasible; but, it will not be simple nor will it be inexpensive. Much will go into the decision-making process. No doubt, in a situation like this, the local department will need help from the outside.

WHEN HOMEGROWN NEEDS HELP

Sometimes You Just Need More

A recent article brought to the fore the concept of taking on *ISIS* and those of its ilk by more than just boots on the ground, fighting deadly wars on their soil and if not successful, those same bloody wars on our own; but to come at them from a third front. That third front is an economic one. This is not a new and revolutionary idea; in the Great War and in WWII it was a strategy of finding ways to eliminate the enemy's ability to keep their economy moving. Bombing factories was as much about destroying systems for manufacturing weapons as it was about displacing the economy of entire regions and eventually countries. The Nazis were defeated by a lack of petrol as much as they were by the onslaught of Allied forces in Europe. There is a very strong argument for fighting the *Islamic State* on a financial battleground. Dry up their funds for weaponry, equipment and personnel and you can defeat an enemy much sooner than by boots on the ground alone.

Louise I. Shelley writes, "Military action alone won't stop the Islamic State. Attack it as a business by cutting off funds and undermining its messaging."[55]

The battles against terrorists whether *lone-wolf* or sent directly from a training camp in Pakistan as part of a larger cell, can be waged as we have outlined in the pages on the home front by men and women of commitment with very specific knowledge about the resources at risk. Battles are key to winning the war and often a war must be fought on multiple fronts. Fronts such as international economic displacement cannot usually be fought on the local level. Those battles require very specific troops and it is in these circumstances that *the homegrown needs help.* Sometimes you just need more.

To win the war you often need more resources, more finances and more human intelligence gathering and boots on the ground. It is not that one particular front is more crucial to the overall success than another anymore than it is about one specific tactic is of greater value. Each has its place. The federal government has resources the locals will never have. Those should be able to enable the feds to conduct and win their battles. However, *their battles* are global in nature whereas the capabilities *and the responsibilities* of the locals are on front lines that include their lawns. Their right to protect their own communities should never be usurped. Assisted by larger agencies *when asked* and *invited in* but never demeaned by brushing aside those who know their communities and their resources better than anyone.

Recall the story of Nehemiah which I related earlier. Nehemiah encouraged the people when their adversaries were strong against them. He said, "Do not be afraid of them. Remember the

Lord, great and awesome and fight for your brethren, your sons, your daughters, your wives and your houses."[56]

This is perhaps the best point at which to remind yourselves, as you study and direct your thoughts toward how you might be able to make this type of a new confederacy of methodologies and mindsets work within your community, it is only by the direction and grace of the God of the Bible such an undertaking can ever hope to succeed. The framers of the U.S. Constitution felt the same way about America and her newly acquired independence. King Solomon, the wisest man ever to live wrote concerning the protection of the homes and cities of Israel around the year 966 BC and the truth of what he wrote still applies today. The New King James Version says it like this: "Unless the Lord builds the house, they labor in vain who build it. Unless the Lord guards the city, the watchman stays awake in vain."[57] The International Standard Version completes the translation this way: "Unless the LORD builds the house, its builders labor uselessly. Unless the LORD guards the city, its security forces keep watch uselessly."[58] You may be one who is completely skeptical of anything *religious*. That's fine because the historicity of the Bible can withstand a good skeptical review of its facts. The history behind what Solomon wrote is solid.

WHEN ENOUGH IS ENOUGH

Have you ever had the unfortunate position of being in grade school and having the class bully completely focused on you, your lunch money, and your milk money or just completely infatuated with humiliating you at recess, usually in front of the prettiest and most popular girl in the class? Perhaps a short anecdote is in order.

We had just such a bully in our school as in every school. He was actually a grade ahead of me. As far as I can recall, I never had any dealings with him but I certainly knew his reputation. Years later when I was a local police officer, he was still the class bully, he persisted in claiming that whenever I had to confront him for breaking the law, I was trying to get revenge for some deed he had done to me in elementary school. He was built like a brick outhouse, vicious and feared. He was also in the elevated ranking of an internationally known bad guys' biker club whose name has to do with evil spirited ambassadors from the underworld.

This particular individual had eluded arrest one weekend even after terrorizing a bar, pushing a local cop and taking another cop's nightstick and using it to break out the light bulbs decorating the rather plain lot full of used cars for sale. The officers who failed to arrest him were graciously given a few days away from the hustle and bustle of police work to reconsider their vocational calling. The very next Friday I respond to another bar where this same individual was creating his own special style of mayhem. The luck of the draw would have me with the same part-time back up partner the officer had the week before... his was an apparently too short a sabbatical. Into the bar I go and there sits my supposed nemesis with a drink in his hand. I told him he was leaving. He said that he would when he finished his beer. I took the beer from his hand and told him he was done. He was unhappy and worse yet he had a large audience. I knew two things. First, I was NOT going to go the way of the officer from the previous week and I knew what was about to happen was going to hurt a great deal. To my surprise, he got up and headed to the door. To my chagrin, he stopped in the doorway, now blocking it, turned and faced me and began to taunt me. I instructed the officer standing next to me to use his Tazer™ on him. When I did not hear the distinctive (and scary) sound of a large number volts of electrical current flowing from device to bad guy and I did not see bad guy falling to the floor in a pile of electrified cannoli, I looked over and, to my dismay, saw only the catatonic face of my *backup* officer. Now I *knew* this was going to hurt.

I was holding in my right hand my PR24™ baton in the position for a close-in body strike. Knowing the list of options had now dwindled to one, I let fly with as much forward thrust as I could manage in that close-in space and made direct contact with the mid-abdomen of this large, drunk, angry individual. I watched in amazement as he dropped to the floor and began sobbing uncontrollably. We drug him to the car, still sobbing. By now my catatonic partner was all prepared to do battle… figures. The big bad bully cried all the way to the station and complained about the tightness of the handcuffs. He ended up back in prison and a few years later, in a leadership coup of his loyal motorcycle cronies, he was killed. At that moment, in that bar, *enough was enough*. I understood the risk and I expected the worst. Thankfully, I was wrong. I had reached a point where this was not going to go on any longer.

America needs to reach that point with ISIS, al Qaeda, every alphabetical derivation of al Qaeda, every wacko like Dylann Roof[59] and say enough is enough. Roof wanted a race war. Some think people formerly in Washington want the same thing. There is craziness all around and people hiding behind political correctness. News media who cannot report a terrorist shooter is also a follower of Islam because it is labeling him, yet he professes it is *his* religion which has driven him to do what he has done or is attempting to do.

It is time for America to stop blaming police for all the bad things that happen in a community and they happen disproportionality to some sections of the community. *Enough is enough.*

There have been calls for police to take on their roles in the manner of firefighters who are reactive not proactive. (I disagree that firefighters are only reactive but that is another story.) The idea is cops should sit at the station and wait for the call of trouble. They should not proactively enforce laws, not even traffic—just stay back out of sight until you are needed. What a crock! If they did that, then the hue and cry would be they were too slow or why did you not get here before you went there? It is too ludicrous to even fathom.

What is needed is the most proactive approach law enforcement has ever taken and it includes specifically chosen persons from the community who have direct connections or knowledge about the local assets that are perceived to be at risk of attack by these either home-grown or internationally trained morons. Communities have the capability to protect their own assets which are at risk. Will they need help sometimes? Yes. Is there help available? The answer will be 'yes' if there are not too many bruised noses and egos. The biggest obstacle to completing this type of a transforming mission is our own reluctance because it has never been done before and that reluctance is magnified by the way in which left wing *main stream* media are prepared to skewer and roast any public official, particularly cops who try to do the right thing and sometimes fail. There could be failure in some of the evaluations or the planning. On such a large-scale project, there is bound to be failure. But failure is only failure if you do not learn from it and you do not get back up and move forward through it.

America, we should attempt this daring new concept. Why? Simply, because we have a lot to lose and if we continue to do what we have always done we will continue to get the results we have always gotten. It is idiocy to think we can keep doing things the same way and get different results! So, we try. We take to heart what was written a century ago by Theodore Roosevelt: that we be the man "...who spends himself in a worthy cause; who, at the best, knows in the end the triumph of high achievement, and who at worst, at least fails while daring greatly, so that his place shall never be with those timid souls who know neither victory or defeat."[60]

HONORING THE BADGE

If you have ever had the occasion to attend the funeral for a law enforcement officer or perhaps visited the National Law Enforcement Memorial in Washington D.C. when they add the newest names of officers slain to the wall of honor, you have witnessed the deep emotion which goes along with honoring those officers. One of the precepts that goes along with honoring the officer is to make mention as to how his or her life and career honored *the badge.* In an earlier chapter of this book were pictures of 19th Century police and sheriff's badges. They were distinct and distinctive whether ornately fashioned or hand stamped on a coin; either was honorable because of what they represent. The badge is also honored by the way it is worn and by the officer who wears it. All alone, the badge is a piece of metal that means literally nothing. There are, in my small collection, some fake marshal's badges in the style of the old west. They were purchased knowing they were imitations and merely for their style. But they have no meaning or honor with them.

When a police officer takes an oath of office, he raises his right hand (and, in my day, places his other hand on the Bible), and makes an oath to uphold and defend the laws of the city, county, state and United States. Because of that oath, the officer is legally empowered to enforce the laws by arresting someone, taking away their freedom *before* they are convicted of a crime. That is a very large responsibility. Our personal freedom in this country is the single most important right we have as Americans. For someone, an official of government, to have the authority to take that freedom from us, they better know the law and must respect the authority they have been given. Their badge is the symbol of that authority. Therefore, it is to be honored by the public and the officer who wears it. It is the single heaviest piece of metal ever worn yet it weighs only a few ounces.

At this time in American history, the honor and respect shown to America's law enforcement is at the lowest point in my recollection and my time dates before the riots against 'the man' in the sixties and seventies of the last century. When I began in law enforcement, many of us wore small tie pins in the shape of a pig. We took the derogatory epithet thrown at us and turned it into Pride Integrity Guts. The slanderous and hateful things said about us in those days' pales in comparison to the crucifying officers are getting today for working hard at doing their job well. It comes in part because a few officers have abused their authority and they should be punished. There is an orchestrated attack against cops, it seems from the left-wing media and many of those currently inside the Beltway and, up until just recently, inside 1600 Pennsylvania Avenue. It is the summer of our discontent. Because of the actions of a few, the lambasting by the media and the heavy handedness of the federal government and against police; perhaps the most discontented are the police themselves. They are discouraged and every single day many of them are ready to walk away. But they don't. They stay.

In the recent James Bond film, *Skyfall*, Bond is shot and presumed dead when he does not return after his body disappeared falling into a river from a train bridge; lethally shot by a high-powered rifle. After hearing of a terrorist attack in London, through a cameo appearance by Wolf Blitzer of CNN, he reappears mysteriously in M's condo. Their dialogue fits here.

James Bond: So, this is it. We're both played out.

M: Well, if you believe that, why did you come back?

James Bond: Good question.

M: Because we're under attack. And you know we need you.

James Bond: Well, I'm here.[61]

That last line, spoken with a heavy sigh, may describe many law enforcement officers' own response when the society's actions are weighing heavily upon them. The rest of the time, however, you will find in any department an eagerness and zeal to go out and do the job, do it well and make a difference. Maybe, in today's world, that sounds a little corny. But, it is the truth.

When it comes time to stretch the Thin Blue Line, there will be people from the community brought into the law enforcement circles who will have strikingly different views about police authority. At times, it could be a volatile mixture. As the lead LEO on the project, you will have to consider before bringing into *the blue* if certain individuals can learn to fit and ask yourself, "Is what they bring to the table sufficient enough to risk a meltdown within the team?" It is not necessary to try to avoid all conflict. Conflict can be constructive and it can be an initiator of growth on both sides. That leads to the question, how to know when to press on and when to exercise the better part of valor by passing.

First, you *must* know the law enforcement members already part of your operation. You must know them inside and out. Leadership demands it. You must be focused on the end goal. You must examine the person you are considering placing into the line to know as best as you can how they might fare in such a dynamic relationship. Is give and take possible or are they too stiff necked? Finally, you consider the value of the expertise they are bringing to the team. If their value is exceptionally high and it is unavailable anywhere else then those who have conflict within the line will have to be reminded what is at stake and put their personal agendas aside. The same is true on both sides of the badge.

Recently, I had published an article in a law enforcement magazine on the role of police in today's world. I posed this question: "Does our society expect these cops, who have been told to go away and not come out until they are called for, to also be the citizens' sole protector?" As I consider what the plausible answers are to that question, I was drawn back to the *Skyfall* movie again when *M* is before their form of a congressional hearing. Perhaps it is best to again let *M* respond to us.

Today I've repeatedly heard how irrelevant my department has become. "Why do we need agents, the Double-0 section? Isn't it all antiquated?" Well, I suppose I see a different world than you do, and the truth is that what I see frightens me. I'm frightened because our enemies are no longer known to us. They do not exist on a map. They're not nations, they're individuals. And look around you. Who do you fear? Can you see a face, a uniform, a flag? No! Our world is not more transparent now, it's more opaque! It's in the shadows. That's where we must do battle. So, before you declare us irrelevant, ask yourselves, how safe do you feel?[62]

THE MEDIA'S ROLE

Perhaps an oxymoron that needs to be addressed within these pages is in the role of effective, proactive criminal justice endeavors the greatest asset any agency can have and the most destructive nemesis any agency can have are exactly one in the same. It is doubtful any local newspaper editor or other media mogul would view themselves in such a negative light and perhaps *destructive nemesis* is a bit heavy handed. More often than not, the newspaper owner or editor would see themselves as the protector of the citizens from those in government who might abuse their power. As an example, the motto for the local newspaper in Canton, Ohio plays off the name of the paper, *The Repository.* The tag line reads: "Truth shall be his guide, the publick good his aim… well-informed men, of all parties, are invited to make it a Repository of their sentiments."[63] If those sentiments and ideals are the goal of public media two hundred years after they were first written, then how is it most media deals in the sensational, the sensual, the sound-bite, and the sales market? The answer is green (usually).

That is not a criticism it is a simple fact. It takes money to run a newspaper particularly in today's digital world. It takes money to pay employees and keep the radio or television station on the air in the midst of competition. Please don't leave here with the idea that I am proposing television, print and on-line media are the new axis of evil! There has been, however, more than a few times when for the sake of sales, public servants have been thrown under the bus and now, those public servants are a bit skeptical of a reporter or editor who wants an interview and the officer can see a local bus schedule sticking out of the reporter's back pocket!

When I began my tenure as Chief of Police for Louisville, Ohio I was told by other chiefs of which news agencies or reporters I should be wary. One of the papers, in general, was from a larger city north of us. As it turned out, I developed an excellent professional working relationship with one specific reporter from that paper. I got to the point where, if I needed very specific information out to the public in a certain way and at a certain time, all I had to do was to call my reporter friend. He would make certain everything went smoothly. I could give him information ahead of the curve to help our cause. Other chiefs swore my reporter friend was not trustworthy. Well, I had a lot of my professional capital sunk into that relationship and it worked. The point is *relationship building* is the only certain way to create the type of working environment for your new centurions. You may want to seriously consider attaching an extremely trustworthy reporter or two to your new Thin Blue Line. It depends largely on the relationship you already have with the media sources and what benefits the reporters would bring to the team. You must require the media masters of the reporters you receive will agree to assign the reporter you choose for whatever indefinite period you set and there can be no trading of players in mid-season without your consent! Also, very specific regulations must be set forth as to the dissemination of information only upon the approval of yourself or some *one* other individual you select. You cannot have a plethora of persons with information release authority. That will bring only disaster.

It is the *Thin Blue Line Project* Law Enforcement Unit Commander's responsibility to educate the new centurions on the principles, purpose, plans, and preparations necessary to make the interdiction work. The Commander must also educate the media which are to be embedded with the centurions on the very same precepts:

PRINCIPLES, PURPOSE, PLANS, AND PREPARATIONS.

Notice that each, with the exception of *purpose,* is plural. The purpose is singular. The principles were first discussed in the section, *Citizen Soldiers/Citizen Cops.* The purpose has been described here as interdicting terrorists or other criminals *before* they can execute their crimes against the community. The plans include the identification of targets and the risk analysis for those targets and the preparations include the training, the evaluation and the practice of the teams to fulfill their team assignments. If you desire an effective and beneficial relationship with your local media, this type of embedded operation is essential. Can it come back to bite you? Absolutely! Just make certain you are up-to-date on all your shots! The Rand Corporation completed a study on the effectiveness of embedded reporters in various military campaigns. They considered it from three viewpoints, the military objectives view; the news media's need for information view; and the public view. An overview of the results of this study are in the following table:

64

Outcomes	Vietnam	Grenada	Panama	1st Gulf War	Somalia	Haiti	Former Yugoslavia	Afghanistan	Iraq
Military									
Operational security	+	++	++	+		–	+	+	–
Legal obligations									
Sufficient press access	+	– – –	–	– –	+	+			+
Public	–	+	+	+	–	–		+	+
Support military mission									
Good public relations									
Public informed	– –	–	–	+	–	–	–		+
Press	–	– –	–	– –	+				+
International	–	–	–	+		+		–	+
Credibility	– –	–	+	+	–				+
Information operations	– –						–		+
Press									
Newsworthy information									
Access	++	– – – –	–	–	+	++	–	–	++
Safety	–	++	+/–	++	–	+	+	+	–
Provide information to the public									
4th Estate obligation									
Market share									
Print									
Television									
"Quality" journalism									
Accuracy									
Credibility	–								–
Public									
Gain information									
Satisfaction	–	+	+	+	–			+	+
Informed	–			+				–	+
Be "well-served"	–/+	–	–	?					?

NOTES: A plus (+) denotes a positive, good, or satisfactory outcome; multiple pluses (++) indicate a *more* positive outcome, both in absolute terms and relative to operations with fewer pluses. A plus and minus (+/–) denotes a mixed outcome or pros and cons. Minuses (–) denote negative, poor, or insufficient outcomes relative to notional reasonably expected standards. Multiple minuses again indicate particularly negative outcomes. Empty cells indicate either neutral outcomes or outcomes for which we lack sufficient information to make a judgment. A question mark (?) indicates an outcome that is open to debate depending on the normative stance taken.
RAND MG200-5.3

Researchers found there were factors both positive and negative in the use of embedded reporters. They wrote, "…our analysis finds that the embedded press system is, in general, likely to produce the greatest number of the most positive outcomes for press-military relations. Note, however, that successful implementation of this system relies on both the press and the military, and it is vulnerable to diminished performance due to many other factors, including limited operational lead time or the nature of the operation. Nor is the embedded press system to be considered a "sure winner" in all future conflicts."[65]

One specific study which also showed an overall positive impact from embedded journalists read as follows. "...the embedded press system, when coupled with unilateral reporting and a credentialing system to protect operational security, is expected to result in positive outcomes in almost every category of evaluation that we consider."[66] The focus of the Rand study was, of course, military in nature. However, the direct implications for a positive impact with the Thin Blue Line project are apparent.

Chapter 4

Bringing it Home II The Sequel

I wrote in the earlier section under *Bringing it Home* the farther one gets from the common, every day Americans, the brothers and sisters of this great nation, the more one tends to define everything, including justice by rank, privilege, power and prestige. We made some comments about how, as important as the federal system can be for manpower and resources; there is a tendency at that level to see everything as being about the federal and very little interest paid to the local. In 2003, the first printing of Terrorism Prevention and Response: *The Definitive Law Enforcement Guide to Prepare for Terrorist Activity* hit the law enforcement community. A quick review of a couple of sections will make the point for us as to how drastically different the thinking behind *Stretching the Thin Blue Line* really is.

Under "Citizen's Reporting Duties" is the following directives: "Citizen participation in the war on crime and domestic terrorism is essential to a secure homeland. Such involvement is best accomplished by the forwarding of information and intelligence gleaned by members of the general public.

SUSPECTED VIOLATIONS OF FEDERAL LAW

- Call local F.B.I. Legal Attaché Office –or-
- Call the F.B.I. tip hotline at 866/483-5137 –or-
- Notify the F.B.I. on the Internet at…." [67]

You get the picture.

The author goes on to describe the *Mission of the American Citizen* and the *Mission of Law Enforcement.* A few examples are noteworthy. Under the Mission of the American Citizen it is divided into *In the Home, In the Community, While Traveling, In Buildings, In Your Heart.* In the home the American citizen is to "Learn about the enemy… its origins, its philosophy, its tactics, its intentions. Discuss current events with your children…Teach your children that sad but true, evil exists in the hearts and minds of some people who hate… Demonstrate pride and loyalty for America… Fly the American flag as often as possible…"[68] I must stop there, I really must.

In the Community, according to the text, there are a couple of good ideas. "Know what is normal for your neighborhood… Be alert to and report suspicious persons, statements, packages… (*and* then comes) Look after one another… Heed the Homeland Security Warnings, Contribute time or money to worthwhile causes… Work to re-elect legislators who pledge to work with the President on matters relating to terrorism and homeland security… Be aware of left-leaning judges who wish to "legislate" from the bench."[69] I put the page number in the *Endnotes* so you could see I'm not making this up. Before I share what the author says about the mission of law enforcement, I must share a couple of examples from *In Your Heart.* "Support the military and law enforcement campaign to fight terrorism. Demonstrate your patriotism in words and deeds. Be prepared to defend your country against those who would disparage it. Whatever your religion or religious beliefs, pray for victory over terrorism, then a lasting peace. **Never forget 9-11.**" (Emphasis in original text)[70]

In the text, under the Mission of Law Enforcement, the author lists some basic concepts that are worthwhile but some, just by themselves without any context leave you to scratch your head and wonder. I will offer just one. "Think like a terrorist in your patrol area; play devil's advocate, seek out vulnerable targets and react accordingly."[71] This book described itself not only as 'The Definitive Law Enforcement Guide to Prepare for Terrorist Activity' it also had emblazoned across the cover RESTRICTED: Sensitive Material for Law Enforcement Use Only (which if that's the case why was there a section on citizen's duties? I digress.)

If we are to *bring home* the concept that we can and must learn new techniques to stop terrorists before they hit us in our local communities we have to pitch the Pablum that had been bottle fed to Americans under the disguise of *real, tactical, effective counter terrorism.* It is time to *get real!*

EXPANDING THE CASTLE DOCTRINE

John Wayne, my favorite actor of all time and who lived up in real life to the image of one of the greatest Americans of all time had some great lines in more movies than I care to count. In the movie on the Allied invasion of Europe in WWII titled, The Longest Day he is a colonel in the 82nd Airborne. Prior to their boarding the planes to head to the drop zones, he addresses his command. He closes by saying, "Your mission tonight is strategic. You can't give the enemy a break. Send 'em to hell."[72]

In this book's *Prologue* was the following statement: The enemy is on our doorstep. You can hunker down in the house, run out the back door to try to escape, or you can open that front door and send the enemy to meet the Judge. **It is time to stop being afraid.** When you think about the castle doctrine in those terms, it is clear enough as you think about it for your own home. What about your son's or daughter's home in another city or state? What about your parent's homes or your neighbors? What about the guy down the block or across town? Are their castles worth you defending them with the same zeal? Now consider your town, your city or maybe your county or state. Wherever you decide to draw the line, make the entire area *your castle*. Draw a line in the sand and double dog dare the enemy to step over it. Then, don't balk like President Obama did in Syria with his line in the sand on the use of chemical weapons. If the enemy crosses your line in the sand, then take a cue from John Wayne as, Col. Kirby – *Your mission is strategic. You can't give the enemy a break. Send 'em to hell.*

CONCLUSION

Local law enforcement teamed with individuals inside their community are the most likely to interdict a terrorist attack on a local resource during the early stages of pre-attack surveillance of the targets. One of the methodologies is to determine what resources in the city are the primary targets. Of the many variables that makes a resource a primary target, or on the flip side of the same coin can keep it totally off the terrorists' radar, is the vulnerability of the target. The harder the target the less likely it will be attacked.

A great deal of distance has been traveled in only a hundred and a half pages. We have talked about the society as a whole and brought it down to a father's leadership in the home. We have considered the mindset of an internationally traveled and trained terrorist and hopefully realized his zeal and commitment to become a martyr for Islam, if that is his chosen cause; because we know there are other terrorists with similar zeal for other causes, is still less than our commitment to keep those who would harm our families the hell out of our castles.

We have shared about how none of this works, whether it is the family unit or the community's new centurions and the reshaped *thin blue line* unless the God of the Bible is behind it. That one sticks in the throat of many folks, maybe even you. I can only report to you what I have witnessed over sixty years of life, forty plus of them connected to law enforcement and that is God's Word is truth and God must be behind what we have said here for it to work is straight from that same truth. I've said all along, though, don't let not understanding God's role in this prevent you from considering the tactics, the concepts, and the planning processes. They are real and they work, *Lord willing*. Read through it again and decide for yourself.

The endgame here is that your community may be sitting on resources some terrorist group wants to destroy, steal or to simply attack to wreak havoc and induce fear and panic. If you are on their target list, don't you think you better have a strategy? Think about this... the one resource every community in America has that terrorists from any group can harm or steal just to create unbridled fear is our children. The next time you cruise past a playground, elementary school or sports field of some kind and you see all those kids playing and laughing; having a great time; imagine what one IED disguised as almost anything would do to those kids and to your community. That alone should have made it worth reading through a mere hundred and sixty pages or so to see if there is *anything* in there which might be able to help you.

Where do you go from here? You read through the book and it seemed to make sense. You can see what resources in your community could be targets but a big part of you is struggling with whether a terrorist would really come to your town. You are so small and there are so many other places a terrorist could hit, why would they come to your place? You can already hear some of the nay-sayers back at your department wondering why you would spend so much time trying to bring in members of the community to work alongside the cops to make sure resources are protected. Those, of course, will be the same people pointing the finger at you when something does go down and it might have been able to be stopped. It may not be an international terrorist. It may be a bunch of drugged out zombies from your town or a town over one who decided they were going to steal what it took to set up their own meth lab and maybe grab some other goodies they don't even know what the uses are so they'll break into the college chemistry buildings. But, what if you didn't listen to the nay-sayers and you went ahead developing the ideas put forth in this book. You've had the night custodian and the maintenance folks from the college on board with you about keeping a tight eye on things and they happened to notice a car in a parking lot a couple of nights in a row that did not have a college sticker on it. They decided to write down the plate and description and give you a call. A stake-out of the building nabbed three felons that have just earned a ride and all expenses paid 3 to 6-year vacation at Pleasure Palace, also known as the state penitentiary. What are the nay-sayers saying now? What has happened to the public perception of your department? The media guys you embedded with your centurions on the blue line, how much did they enjoy getting that story first hand? How much good-will did that buy you with the media overall?

Perhaps, if you follow the concepts in this book, a terrorist or even Billy-Bad-Boy will never show up during your watch. Maybe it is because you were able to harden the targets and they by-passed them. That is a success you could have you'll never know about. How about the impact you have been able to have in your own home or in the homes of some of your officers? Have you opened up the door for more men in your circle of influence to be better fathers? If so, I'd say this book has been worth your time.

While I was a police officer and then as a Chief of Police, I knew that with the decisions I made, no matter how I went with the decision were going to be me for the rest of my life and I would have to face myself in the mirror every morning. That is a tough enough assignment just with aging. But I wanted to be able to be retired and never have a regret when I looked in the mirror about something I could have done that I didn't. Did I make mistakes? Sure! Probably dozens! In the end, that wasn't what mattered. If you can end your tour of duty and there was never a serious terrorist attack, homegrown or otherwise, or you had an attempt and you were able to interdict it, then you end your tour with your head high. Thankful that your officers and staff, your volunteers and community members all came together and when all was said and done, the game ended with the Good Guys 1 Bad Guys 0. If you are wise, you will either bow your head or look heavenward and say, "Thanks." If it was your watch, you gave it everything you had and still the enemy got through, then, do not hang your head in despair, though grief will come. Rather, understand the God of all heaven and earth does not explain why He allows to happen what happens and rest in knowing you are not Him. Then:

Rescue the injured

Resuscitate the critical

Remove the debris

Rebuild what was

Remember who sacrificed so that those who remain can

Resume the battle

May the God of the Bible, His only Son, Jesus Christ and the Holy Spirit give you the faith to trust Him as you forge ahead in the battle one more day.

ENDNOTES

(Endnotes)

1   http://www.jrj-socrates.com/cartoon%20pages/jay_ward.htm

2   http://www.heritage.org/research/commentary/2007/07/the-american-experiment

3   http://list25.com/25-most-notorious-outlaws-of-the-wild-west/

4   http://list25.com/25-most-notorious-outlaws-of-the-wild-west/

5   http://www.georgiaencyclopedia.org/articles/history-archaeology/john-henry-doc-holliday-1851-1887

6   https://sites.google.com/site/19thcenturyoldwestoutlaws/wyatt-earp-an-outlaw

7   http://en.wikipedia.org/wiki/Jesse_James

8   www.snyderstreasures.com

9   http://www.texasranger.org/history/HistoricBadges.htm

10   http://armsaandthlw.com/archives/2011/03/court_court_ruling_on.php

11   https://www.biblegateway.com/passage/?search=-John+15:13

12   President James Marshall" *Air Force One* – Century City

13   http://www.imdb.com/title/tt0083131/

14   http://www.snopes.com/quotes/internet.asp#YqRR-go2WDesjcfsH.99

15   Cohan, George M. "Over There" 1917

16   http://www.gr0wing.com/3-core-habits-keep-mind-strong-chaos/

17   http://offgridsurvival.com/entirepowergrid-cyberattack/

18   http://www.Newsmax.com/Newsfront/rogers-cyberat-tacks-us-infrastructure/2014/11/20/id/608634/#ixzz-3JyOoOo6p

19   http://www.cdc.gov/nchs/fastats/marriage-divorce.htm

20   http://ijhssnet.com/journals/Vol_3_No_8_Special_Is-sue_April_2013/26.pdf

21   http://www.nytimes.com/1989/01/24/science/sad-lega-cy-of-abuse-the-search-for-remedies.html

22   http://www.dailymail.co.uk/news/article-2253421/1-3-US-children-live-father-according-census-number-par-ent-households-decreases-1-2-million.html

23   http://datacenter.kidscount.org/data/tables/107-chil-dren-in-single-parent-families-by#detailed/1/any/fal se/868,867,133,38,35/10,168,9,12,1,13,185/432,431

24   http://scps.nyu.edu/export/sites/scps/pdf/global-affairs/marta-sparago.pdf

25   https://www.trackingterrorism.org/article/psycholo-gy-recruiting-terrorists

26   https://www.biblegateway.com/passage/?search=James-+2%3A14-26&version=NKJV;NIV

27   http://biblehub.com/romans/13-4.htm

28   http://www.freerepublic.com/focus/f-religion/2865360/
      posts

29   http://biblehub.com/hebrews/10-25.htm

30   http://www.weeklystorybook.com/comic_strip_of_the_
      daycom/2010/05/saturday-profile-chris-browne-on-
      hagar-the-horrible.htm

31   http://hagarthehorrible.com/2014/04/10/imag-
      ine-dragons/

32   http://biblehub.com/matthew/5-17.htm

33   Ibid.

34   http://freebeacon.com/national-security/report-islam-
      ic-state-claims-radioactive-device-now-in-europe/

35   http://southaven.org/252/Community-Programs

36   http://aliens.wikia.com/wiki/C18_Locker_Aliens

37   Belhadj, Joshua "Anticipating Urban Evacuations: A
      Planning Support System for Impact Reduction" Uni-
      versity of Cincinnati, College of DAAP, School of Plan-
      ning 2007

38   Ibid.

39   Belhadj, Joshua S., "Anticipating Urban Evacuations: A
      Planning Support System for Impact Reductions" Uni-
      versity of Cincinnati: Feb. 17, 2008

40   https://maps.yahoo.com/place/?lat=40.7649414124685
      &lon=-73.97575378417969&q=Manhattan%2C NY
      United States

41   Riggs, Ross L. "In Times of Crisis: Developing Con-
      tingency Management Teams for Missionary Sending
      Churches and Agencies" Baptist Bible Seminary, Clarks

Summit, PA: 2006

42   http://www.washingtontimes.com/news/2013/oct/31/
inside-china-nuclear-submarines-capable-of-widespr/

43   Belhadj, Joshua "Anticipating Urban Evacuations: A
Planning Support System for Impact Reduction" University of Cincinnati, College of DAAP, School of Planning 2007 (Including NIPP and ESIR equations)

44   http://www.shinola.com/shop/black-shoe-polish.html

45   www.USConstitution.org

46   http://www.factcheck.org/2009/05/misquoting-yama-
moto/

47   http://extranosalley.com/?p=37400

48   Riggs, Daniel personal photo 27 May 2015

49   http://faculty.frostburg.edu/rpm/rkauffman/pdf_files/
thin_blue_line.pdf

50   http://www.endangeredspeciesinternational.org/in-
sects5.html

51   http://www.worldatlas.com/webimage/countrys/africa/
sc.htm

52   http://www.worldpoliticsreview.com/articles/4100/
the-powell-doctrines-enduring-relevance

53   "Breakout at the Border" NEWSMAX, June 2015

54   http://faculty.frostburg.edu/rpm/rkauffman/pdf_files/
thin_blue_line.pdf

55   Shelley, Louise I. "Criminal Minds" *The American Le-
gion,* June 2015

56   Nehemiah 4:14, Holy Bible, NKJV, Broadman & Hol-

man Publishers; Nashville 1985

57 Psalm 127:1, Holy Bible, NKJV, Broadman & Holman Publishers; Nashville 1985

58 http://biblehub.com/psalms/127-1.htm

59 http://www.foxnews.com/us/2015/06/18/dylann-roof-suspect-in-deadly-charleston-shooting-introvert/

60 Roosevelt, Theodore *The Critic*, personal copy.

61 http://www.imdb.com/title/tt1074638/quotes

62 http://www.imdb.com/title/tt1074638/quotes

63 Saxton, John The Repository Vol. 1 No. 1, March 30, 1815 (Founder's Statement)

64 http://www.rand.org/content/dam/rand/pubs/monographs/2004/RAND_MG200.pdf p 99

65 Ibid. p 108

66 Ibid. p 110

67 Mariani, Cliff Terrorism Prevention and Response Looseleaf Law Publications: Flushing NY 2003 p 21

68 Ibid. p 92

69 Ibid. p 93

70 Ibid. p 94

71 Ibid. p 95

72 http://independentfilmnewsandmedia.com/the-longest-day-send-em-to-hell-john-wayne/

363.2 – RIG

Riggs, Ross L.

Stretching the thin blue line.

CHAPTER 3 141

LOCALLY OWNED

CHAPTER 4 165

BRINGING IT HOME II THE SEQUEL

ENDNOTES. 173

CONTENTS